Unstoppable

The Art of Goal Crushing with
Confidence, Resilience, and Motivation

Jamesha Ross, MBA, BSN, RN

Unstoppable
© 2022 by Jamesha Ross. All rights reserved.

Published by Author Academy Elite
PO Box 43, Powell, OH 43065
www.AuthorAcademyElite.com

All rights reserved. This book contains material protected under international and federal copyright laws and treaties. Any unauthorized reprint or use of this material is prohibited. No part of this book may be reproduced or transmitted in any form or by any means, electronic or mechanical, including photocopying, recording, or by any information storage and retrieval system, without express written permission from the author.

Identifiers:
LCCN: 2022901150
ISBN: 979-8-88583-000-3 (paperback)
ISBN: 979-8-88583-001-0 (hardback)
ISBN: 979-8-88583-002-7 (ebook)

Available in paperback, hardback, e-book, and audiobook

Any Internet addresses (websites, blogs, etc.) and telephone numbers printed in this book are offered as a resource. They are not intended in any way to be or imply an endorsement by Author Academy Elite, nor does Author Academy Elite vouch for the content of these sites and numbers for the life of this book.

Some names and identifying details have been changed to protect the privacy of individuals.

Part 1, Part 2, and Part 3 illustrations by Armani Reed.

This book is dedicated to my grandmother, Osrine, and oldest daughter, Shella. You gave me strength and taught me that my why is bigger than me.

Contents

Part 1   Survival Mode

Chapter 1   What Is Survival Mode?................3

Chapter 2   What the S?!...........................23

Part 2   Self-Awareness

Chapter 3   Who Am I?...........................35

Chapter 4   Visions and Goals: Personal and Professional...46

Part 3   Crushing It

Chapter 5   Busy Being Busy......................55

Chapter 6   Self-Care Matters.....................61

Chapter 7   Confidence..........................66

Chapter 8   Resilience 74

Chapter 9   Motivation 97

Chapter 10 Inspire: Your Highest Level of Success 106

About the Author 117

Notes 119

PART 1

Survival Mode

I was at a conference in Tampa, Florida, when I first heard the quote that's often incorrectly attributed to Albert Einstein, but it's traced to Rita Mae Brown: "Insanity is doing the same thing over and over again, but expecting different results." A mental light bulb flashed brightly; I needed to change something or maybe change everything if I wanted my life to be different.

Be honest with yourself as read you Part 1 and consider what might need to change *for you*. What is going on in your life right now? What is keeping you up at night? Are you doing the same thing and expecting different results? Are you in survival mode now, or have you leaped out? Spoiler alert: It is what it is. All of us have faced some form of survival mode, but we may not have recognized it.

CHAPTER 1

What Is Survival Mode?

True living breeds moments of clarity and discovery. Growth dances around these moments, and we change as a result of truly living. What causes growth? Is it a choice to grow, or does it happen involuntarily? Growth can be physical, mental, spiritual, and emotional. This book is about growing when you're not supposed to or even trying to. When we face life events that snatch us into survival mode, we have to decide whether we're going to stay put and get used to it or elevate to the next level in life . . . your best life. I want to challenge your beliefs about what success is to you and what you think your best version is. Are you ready? Let's do this.

Success is complex and has many meanings. Think of the complexity of the human body. Our bodies require many systems to work together for one common goal: sustain life. Each system has a distinct purpose and is critical to the body's overall function. These systems are so intricate that they can compensate for each other. When one system is not performing well, another one can adapt and cover for suboptimal performance. Success has different meanings to everyone. Some people feel that success is accumulating material things. Even though its meaning is fluid, I define ultimate success as being able to inspire others and leave a legacy. What will people say about you when you are no longer here? Will you leave a good or bad legacy?

Success is the result of confidence, resilience, and motivation overlapping and working together. Each of these elements can compensate for each other in the same respect as our bodies to maintain life. For example, when your blood pressure decreases, your heart rate will increase to meet the demands of your organs. Another example is when your body temperature elevates, you start sweating to cool your body down. The evaporation of sweat is our body's cooling mechanism. Our bodies will compensate, regulating and maintaining the proper body temperature.

Living within the boundaries of your best version of yourself is a balancing act of direct and indirect actions. The art of living your best life is intentional but subtle. It is in every fiber of you. It is the undercurrent of daily interactions and reactions. Each action is affecting your best version. I'm not saying that you won't have times within this life when you won't feel like you are within your best version. You will appreciate each day and learn from each experience with an understanding that you can learn and grow from everything: the good, the bad, and the messy. Yes, there is something to gain from what feels like a mess. As you progress on your success journey, eventually, you will be able to spot messes from a mile away. It will be similar to seeing an ambulance weaving through traffic. When you see it, you stop and move out of the way. Not only do I stop, but I pray that the person waiting for the ambulance or in the ambulance has the full armor of God covering them. Then I yell for everyone on the road to get out of the way. I know—don't judge me.

I was my grandmother's heartbeat and the sparkle in my grandfather's eye. I was everyone's favorite. It was easy for me to please others. My mother was a workaholic, and my dad was a deadbeat. My mother's long work hours led me to spend a great deal of time at my grandmother's house with my grandmother and cousins. My father's absence may have triggered my grandfather to step up and be the support of a father figure even though he was dealing with the residual of a stroke and required the assistance of others to do simple things. I am the product of my environment laced with a broken family and weaved with high expectations from my grandparents. My grandmother and grandfather were my superheroes.

Look for the shy, medium-height, skinny girl with long, permed hair that sat in the back of the classroom who didn't study much but stayed on the honor roll: that's where you would find me. The only thing required to keep out of trouble was a good report card. I was able to do that with ease. My grades allowed me to have the freedom to do other things; some of those things made life hard for me. I stayed off the radar but managed to surprise everyone when I became pregnant at fourteen and delivered one month after my fifteenth birthday.

I survived child abuse, gang violence, domestic violence, and teenage pregnancy to become more than society said I would be. Society tries to put you in a box or mold, but I learned the cheat code to break the box and the mold. I learned how to play the game of life with my own rules and live my best life. My life, not anyone else's life. Your life is yours, and you can only strive to be the best version of yourself. There is no judgment here. I've seen some dark times and didn't see how I was going to get to the light. Sometimes, the light was the headlight to a huge, fast train.

There is an old saying: "Pressure breaks pipes," and I know now that pressure can break people too. This book will teach you how to be confident, resilient, and motivated when you are supposed to fold under pressure. It's important for the woman who wants more in life but feels stuck and overwhelmed while being pulled in a million directions. This woman wears many hats and doesn't feel confident or strong all the time, but everyone leans on her and expects her to fix everything. At times, the pressure to fix everything all the time or have the answer for the problems that come your way leads to exhaustion. I was able to pull myself out of this quicksand of problems and prevent myself from being stuck. I want to share what I have used over and over to get started, stay motivated, and crush my goals. Living your best life is about making subtle moves that accumulate and maintain the perfect balance of confidence, resilience, and motivation to achieve your ultimate success.

Survival mode looks different for each person and evolves with maturity and experience of the lessons of life. Survival mode is a different definition for a teenager versus a middle-aged woman. It's based on different needs for each phase in life that results in a difference in how we prioritize and respond. When you are in survival mode, you focus your efforts on getting through the day, and there's no effort put into the future. At times, this feels like burnout, and every day is a bad day. During survival mode, tomorrow feels like it's an eternity away. Have you ever come home from a long day of hard, back-breaking work, and before you open the front door, you start praying to yourself, "Lord, please do not let the electricity be off?" After slowly opening the door, you look for signs of electricity. When you see none, you hold your breath, flip the light switch, and the light comes on. Your eyes close as you bow your head, and "thank you, Jesus" softly rolls off your lips. Now, you just have to survive with electricity until tomorrow, payday, and are nervous all night. There is no progress or hope in survival mode. It's very similar to a hamster running on the wheel. There's lots of work being done and effort but no traction, and you're definitely not going anywhere. Overworked and overwhelmed are common emotions when you're in the thick of it.

It becomes so routine for some people that they don't recognize it and therefore do nothing to get out of survival mode. Have you ever been hit in the face with a horrible stench of a dead mouse when you walked into the house? You might start looking for the source of that foul odor. Most people would start with the trash can to find the spoiled food to remove it from the house. But if you find out through the process of elimination that a mouse had gained its wings somewhere in the house, you know it's going to be a long haul of foulness. The people who've been in the house all day seem to be immune to the smell. They seem immune to the smell of rotten death mixed with bowel juice odors floating in the air. It's only when someone comes into the house and questions the scent they become aware of it. The moral to the story is that if you stay in a room with funky, foul odors too long, you can't smell it.

It's the very same concept with survival mode. If you're in survival mode too long, you'll get used to it, and it'll take someone from the outside looking in to take notice and bring it to your attention. Another scenario that could allow you to recognize survival mode is if you are temporarily removed from it then return to it. An illness might force you to take a break due to a health condition, or you may go out of town. Something causes your usual business to be interrupted. The same thing would happen in the rotten food example. If you were to leave the kitchen and go outside, then return to the kitchen, your nose would alert you of the foul odor. However, some people recognize survival mode, and they're okay with it. It feels normal and brings comfort.

Being in survival mode reveals if you're trained to go (TTG) or trained to stay (TTS). A TTGer will quickly come up with a plan to get out of survival mode. A TTSer will plan on staying in survival mode. I'll go into more details about the breakdown of survival mode in the next chapter to help you recognize it creeping into your life.

Here are some examples of what I have survived in my personal and professional life:

Teenage Pregnancy

I tried to hide my pregnancy because I was a good girl. Good girls don't have sex or get pregnant. When you are everyone's favorite, there's a duty to stay at the top. Being quiet and sneaky, I avoided getting attention for things that would change the way my family knew me. I was an honor roll student because learning came easy for me. Once I understood the topic, I was good to go for classwork and testing. Challenges motivated me, and I was eager to learn. I knew I didn't want to be a teenage mother. Having seen girls at the bus stop with strollers, I knew I didn't want that life. But I was naïve and believed my boyfriend when he told me he wasn't going to get me pregnant. I didn't know he had no control over that without protection. I was in love, and he could do no wrong. The summer between eighth grade and ninth grade, I became pregnant at fourteen. Without any skills, I knew I had to work. I lied about my age and got a job as a house cleaner, but I was too young to drive, so I walked to work and rode with my cleaning partner to the assigned houses. I was able to make a little bit of money for a few months.

Without money, I remember starving to death at work. The only option for me was to work with my stomach growling and eat once I returned home. It was a true test of how long I could go without eating because I was in survival mode for both myself and my unborn child. I delivered ten weeks early. My daughter was three pounds, two ounces; she fit in the palm of my small hand! She was barely alive, requiring a tube in her mouth to breathe for her and one in her nose to feed her. She was fighting every minute to be here. When it was time for me to be discharged, I had to leave my precious baby in the hospital. On the day of my discharge, I barely made it to the elevator before my emotions (and hormones) overtook me. The tears didn't stop until I finally passed out in my bed from exhaustion. Would my daughter miss me? Be looking for me? I was scared for her, which temporarily overtook the fear of being a teen mom. Without fail, I visited her every day, and it took all the strength I could muster to hit that elevator button to return home each night. Somehow, though, I survived teen pregnancy and parenting a preemie.

My boyfriend and I would go to the hospital to see our premature daughter every day in the neonatal intensive care unit (NICU). It was intimidating for us, but we knew the skilled staff who worked in the NICU was the only reason our daughter was alive after being born ten weeks early. Family members would come when they could, but we had to go every day no matter what came up. She belonged to us.

Then the day came when I had to go alone. I cried the whole time because my boyfriend was arrested and wasn't going to be released anytime soon. I was alone to do what my daughter needed me to do: be her mother. I was terrified I would hurt her. She could only be touched during feedings or changings through a small circular window in the incubator. Tears are falling as I am writing this because that time in my life was so unpredictable. I was hoping for progress each day but preparing myself for setbacks.

Finally, after a long month, I was allowed to hold her. When that time came, I felt inadequate; I didn't want to be the source of any setbacks. The nurses took the time to teach me, show me, empower me, and help me be her mother. They cared for us so much that before I left, they made me promise that if I needed anything—diapers or formula—to come back to the NICU.

I gained confidence, and in no time, I was doing everything. My baby girl was released home once she weighed five pounds. Before that happened, I had to learn CPR and stay the night with her in a hospital room before she could go home with me. The last night in the hospital was our first night alone. My heart was beating like a drum each time that I checked for the rise and fall of her chest. Light sleeping and heightened senses were my focus. The roller coaster of happiness, fear, and anxiety of that night is etched in my memory. Without a doubt, the nurses were concerned about this five-pound baby girl going home with a fifteen-year-old mother.

Make a note of the people preparing you and giving you tools in those moments of survival. The nurses empowered me to develop my skills as a mother when I had no clue of what to do as a fifteen-year-old mother of a neonate who was fighting for her premature life. Those nurses made a difference in my life. I will never forget one particular nurse who always greeted me with kindness. She was a short stature African American with a very short fade haircut and crisp scrubs. Her smile filled the unit and filled me with strength. The grace and care of the NICU nurses planted a seed in me to become a caring and graceful nurse. I wanted to make a difference in someone else's life. I wanted to make someone feel strong and hopeful.

When you really think about who has been close to you or around you during trying moments, who comes to mind? What did they do to help you? Was it something that they said or did? Take a moment to reflect on that. Now, did that create an urge in you to do something? Did it influence you to take action or not take action? Unfortunately, I have no way of finding the nurse who made a huge impact on me. I encourage you to reach out and contact the person who you've identified, if possible. Let them know the impact they had on you. Give them credit. This may help them to know and inspire them or confirm their purpose.

Another moment of growth for me was the first time I went to the doctor's office with my daughter; I was alone. I realized I had to be the adult in every situation with her. Up until the moment I brought her home, I was in the child role. I was a teenager torn between two roles, and I was most comfortable with the one I couldn't be anymore. I was a mom of a precious, perfect little girl. I had to become her parent.

My early high school years were a mixture of childhood and adulthood for me—my pregnancy and first year of motherhood were during my freshman and sophomore years. As a pregnant and parenting teen, I had more responsibility and real-life issues before I was a legal adult. There wasn't any time to enjoy the "normal" high school experience. Working, doing schoolwork, and enjoying my bundle of joy consumed all my time. Going to school felt like a chore—I felt out of place and wanted it to be over. I was ready for the real world. Or so I thought.

After I gave birth, I was homeschooled for a few months to keep my grades up. My family and I decided it would be better for me to go to the Margaret Hudson Program. It was a school for pregnant and parenting teens with an onsite daycare. The delivery model included education combined with social services for students and their children.

I learned so much at that school about parenting and my body. Along with the supportive nurses and staff, I gained lifelong friendships with some of the students. We were growing into young ladies together, often cooking meals together and sharing food at lunch.

I transferred to my assigned high school in the tenth grade—the pride of North Tulsa, Booker T. Washington High School. I was not like the other kids at my high school; I had real responsibility. I had to consciously decide every day if I wanted to finish high school. I was usually up late with my daughter studying, and I worked as a waitress after school to support her.

I often thought I didn't need anyone to tell me what to do or hold me accountable. My best friend seemed to embody this ideal, and I used to compare my family to hers. She had a lot of freedom because her mom worked as a private duty home health aide. Her mom lived with her clients and came home occasionally. My friend was home alone with her adult sisters and brothers, which allowed her to do what she wanted. Her life was perfect in my fourteen-year-old eyes. She was never in trouble and could stay home from school whenever she wanted to. Boys came over to her apartment all the time, and she always had money.

One day, I decided to run away to her apartment. I was fed up with the rules of my life, and I wanted her freedom. The following day, my aunt came to my friend's apartment fully dressed in her police uniform, knocking like she was the police. Everyone in the apartment feared the police. They weren't used to the police coming over, and some things in the apartment would have created a criminal case. When my aunt demanded to see me, they were more than willing to give me up and let me know I was unwelcome if I was going to cause the police to come to their home. When I saw my aunt's face, I knew she meant business. She fussed at me the whole ride back to my house. I was totally pissed my family was interfering with my quest for freedom. Knowing what I know now, my family was only doing what was required to keep me on track.

There were mornings I thought I wasn't going to school. After telling my mother I wasn't going to school, she would call my grandmother and my aunts. Everyone would come over and get in my personal space like an old lady gang. After that, I was ready to go to school to get peace away from them. Strong women who wanted me to succeed surrounded me. My grandmother always used to tell me that the sky was the limit, and I could do anything if I set my mind to it. It takes a village to raise a child.

At times, it was clear that other parents didn't want their daughters to get *accidentally* pregnant due to being friends with me. One of my classmates stopped hanging with me after her mother found out. At first, she became distant but gradually started ignoring me. I could tell that the long line of questions from her mother about my daughter had a hidden agenda. The questions felt judgmental. I started to feel ashamed and thought that maybe I should not share my daughter with everyone, but that didn't feel right. She is a source of pride, not shame. She was my motivation. I didn't let it get to me because I knew who I was, and my daughter was only part of it.

I moved out of my mother's home my senior year. It was even more challenging that year to go to school than it had been when I lived with my mother. I managed a household, cared for my daughter, held a job, and had to finish high school. One night shortly after I moved into my apartment, there was a knock on my door. The young lady's screams were tearing the door down. She was pleading for me to let her in and to call the police. Her boyfriend had been beating her for hours in her apartment, but she was finally able to escape by jumping from the balcony. However, when she jumped, he grabbed her arm and broke it in the process. That was scary for me to hear on the other side of my door. I was scared for her, myself, and my daughter, but it was the welcome I received from Sun Garden Apartments, a.k.a. Gun Garden, because of the frequent murders and shootings. I managed to survive there for a year until my section 8 voucher was approved.

Other students at my school only had to worry about games, dances, and grades. I had that and much more. I knew I wanted to go to college to avoid a life of struggle. It was just another day in my life to have the water or gas being turned off or my car being repossessed. I wanted more.

Society said otherwise; a black teen mom was supposed to be a high school dropout and on government assistance forever. But when there's a God who has your back, you know otherwise. I survived. I am not putting down anyone who dropped out because I know people who dropped out of high school and later obtained their GED. They made the best decision possible at that time.

I had the support and resources to stay in school and graduate on time. The government assistance programs are for people who need them. I used to be on TANF, section 8, food stamps, title 19 insurance, and daycare assistance. The system was set up to make it easy to stay on those programs and hard to transition to self-sufficiency. I had other plans and decided to do what was harder at the moment to have an easier life later. I knew I didn't want to be using those programs for the rest of my life, so I made decisions that would allow me to get off the programs. Because of my determination, I was able to get off of all of the programs immediately after accepting my first nursing job.

I encourage you to take advantage of any community resources and government assistance programs you qualify for as you navigate survival mode. These programs are for survival mode. Just stick to your plan to succeed, and you'll be able to stand on your own eventually. Take a moment to explore what you need help with and what programs are available to assist. Apply for the assistance and use it as long as you need to. I repeat: these programs are for survival mode, but you won't be in survival mode forever because this book will help you master your ultimate success.

If you have experienced teenage pregnancy or know someone who has experienced it, you understand the complexity of being an adult while being a child. All of a sudden, you're expected to care for a baby and put their needs before yours. Unconditional love determines your every thought and move. The transformation from childhood to adulthood happens too early and within a split second. It shapes the rest of your life. Your body changes when it is not supposed to, and you're forced to adapt. It doesn't feel like an accomplishment while you are living it, but when you make it to your high school graduation, the sense of completion can emotionally overwhelm you. You start to reflect on the daily decisions and challenging moments when your baby wouldn't go to sleep, and you only had three hours before the alarm went off. The only thing that gets you through those crucial moments is your "why." (We'll talk about your why in Part Two.)

Completing high school with teenage pregnancy is a powerful experience that makes you stronger, determined, and unstoppable. It's like an unspoken club. All of the club members developed and earned survival skills and know the "S's." (The S's will be broken down in the next chapter.) You're not alone. Members are plentiful.

Gang Violence

As a teenager, you pretty much know everything you need to know. You only need your family for monetary support, your friends will be there forever, you have life figured out, and nothing is ever going to happen to you. That's for other people, right? *Wrong.* Just wait.

I was very excited to have my really used baby blue Chevy Celebrity. My grandfather helped me get it. He was always doing things, even if it wasn't right, to make his grandkids smile. Life was good! My daughter was one year old, and I was sixteen with wheels. I was still living with my mother, and she agreed to let me spend the night at my friend's house. She only gave me one direction: do not go anywhere else. Yeah, yeah, yeah.

As soon as I arrived at my friend's house, the party plot was set in motion. I was free. I could do whatever I wanted, and partying was at the top of my to-do list. I did feel a micro amount of guilt for disobeying my mother, but the anticipation of fun drowned it out. My friend, her older sister, her older sister's friend, and I were singing and dancing as we posed in the mirror with our jean outfits and short sets. After we were cute and we knew it, we were cruising down the street with music blaring and windows rolled down. Once we arrived at the party, we were in the middle of a sea of youngsters. Couples were dancing all around the dark dance floor. I was able to focus on me and not any responsibility. We danced and laughed from the moment we entered the building until the lights came on.

Finally, the party started breaking up, so the four of us jumped into my car and punched it to the new neighborhood convenience store. Apparently, other people had the same idea. Each vehicle was bumper to bumper with barely enough walking room to mingle. As a new driver, I was nervous to be that close to other vehicles. One wrong move would be a wreck. I was a master of playing it cool when I was nervous. This crowd was a little older than the party crowd. I didn't recognize anyone.

People started getting out and walking around and chatting over the loud music with people stuck in their cars. A tall, heavy-set guy who was dressed in blue walked up to the passenger back window and started talking to my friend's sister. He appeared to be comfortable mingling in the maze of cars. I wasn't paying much attention to their conversation, but they both were smiling as I turned around to see if I could back up because I was blocking the gas pump. As soon as I turned back to the front, my head jolted with a thumping sensation. I felt the back of my head become extremely cold and wet. Before I could process anything, my friend yelled for me to get down. The steering wheel blocked me, but I kept shifting and twisting myself downward until I reached the floor. I could feel my car rolling and bump into the car in front of me. It finally registered that my foot was no longer on the brake pedal. Suddenly, loud popping sounds that sounded like fireworks going off filled my ears. Once the popping sounds stopped, I touched the back of my head and gently rubbed my fingertips over the cold, wet spot. I was bleeding but not in pain. "I've been hit," I said to my friend without emotion.

Her eyes opened widely, and her voice trembled. "You've been shot!" I could feel the wetness extend down the back of my shirt. As I inched my head up from below the seat, I could see the chaos of people running, abandoned cars, and cars fleeing out of the parking lot. My friend jumped out of the passenger door and ran around the back of the car to the driver's side and pressed the gas pedal to the floor as I moved to the passenger seat. I was praying that the shooting was over and that I would be able to see my daughter again. I don't know how we were able to get out of the parking lot, but my friend jumped into action and managed to get us away from the scene.

We had to get to the hospital, but we didn't know how to get there. There was a hospital downtown, but that was all we were sure of. As we were weaving through the streets to find the hospital, we noticed that my friend's older sister was sitting up in the back seat, her head leaning back on the headrest. We kept calling her name, but she didn't answer. Screaming and driving super-fast toward downtown, we knew that we needed to check her pulse, but we didn't know how to do it. A policeman was parked in a parking lot, and we started honking the horn. He didn't respond to our attempts to get his attention. Stopping for help wasn't an option because we knew we had to get to the hospital fast.

Finally arriving at the front entrance of Tulsa Regional Hospital, three of us got out and ran to the door only to find it was locked. We started jumping and waving our arms to the security camera. Someone finally came to the door. Hospital workers went to get my friend's sister out of the car while we were ushered to the emergency room to be checked out. They put me in a curtained area to wait for a doctor while they wheeled my friend's sister into the bay next to mine. I remember shivering as I peeked through the curtain and saw her lying on the stretcher with her clothes cut up and hanging off her. She was not moving, and her body seemed lifeless. My heart pounded as I watched the ER team surround her and place medical equipment on her, but I had a sense of calmness. I thought she would be okay. She *had* to be okay. We are always okay at this age. As I said before, everything that happens only happens to other people.

Unlike my friend's sister who died shortly after the shooting, I was lucky and only received three stitches in the back of my head. I'll never know if I was hit by shattered glass or grazed by a bullet. What I do know is it wasn't my time to go. God protected me. I could not stand to think about leaving my daughter at one year old. She had to fight to be here, and I needed to be with each precious moment of growth: first steps, first day of school, first heart break, first graduation, first fight, and when she becomes a mother. She wouldn't remember me if I left her at one year old. Her father could not raise her without me. My mother would have been stressed to the max with the added responsibility of raising my daughter. Wait, I still had to deal with my mother. I disobeyed her, and I wasn't making the best decision for myself or my daughter. When my mother arrived at the emergency room, she didn't have to say anything. Her face was a mixture of anger and relief as her eyes pierced through my soul. I can only imagine all the things that were going through her mind.

That night was a night of firsts. It was my first time hearing gunshots, being in the middle of a gang shootout, seeing white brain matter, and dealing with death. When the police released my car from storage, it only took a sniffle of air to burn your nostrils and force you to stop breathing. It was the smell of death.

I think this tragedy caused my family to rethink how we handled each other. My grandmother said to me shortly afterward, "You are still here because you are supposed to be. You have not completed the tasks God has assigned to you." I truly believe that everything happens for a reason, and we have to find our lesson in each situation. I learned that being in the wrong place at the wrong time can take your life. What if I'd obeyed my mother? If we had stayed at my friend's house, we would've avoided being in the middle of a gang shoot-out. That was a harsh lesson as a teenager. It was hard to be in crowds after that. I was always looking for a way out when I went to public places. Knowing my exit path was how I coped with my newfound anxiety. I jump whenever I hear loud pops or tailpipes backfiring. I'm terrified of guns. I usually leave parties or gatherings early, and I have to know where the troublemakers are so that I can stay away. I survived gang violence.

Surviving a tragedy changes you. In many ways, it can make you numb to pain. Being so close to death at a young age made me question things. What's my purpose? What am I supposed to be doing? I had to slow down and start paying attention to what was happening in my life. Doors opening and opportunities falling into my lap organically predicted my next step. It always felt right, and I was able to move based on the momentum that was building in my life.

I often share those two life lessons with people to help them understand that you can make something out of nothing no matter where you come from or what you've been through if you have the determination to do so. Teenage pregnancy and gang violence can be life-altering situations that leave few options if you survive. Only a true mindset of determination can pull you through tons of obstacles and chaos that are out of your control. Each time life knocked me down, I used a simple method to get back up. I will be going into detail so that you can use this same method. Each challenge and struggle is preparing you for greatness. Embrace those times when you feel like it's just too damn much. Those are moments of discovery. You learn what your strengths and weaknesses are and what's important to you. Once you find yourself taking note of how great you are and what you need to work on, you can start formulating your self-assessment. Without those real moments, you can only hope that you would do certain things or respond in an acceptable manner. Family first means you need to understand how your decisions will impact your family. You have something to contribute to your family and the world.

Child Abuse

Another family lesson that I want to discuss is the need to shed light on dark family issues. Some family experiences are so dark and sickening that it is hard to allow the memories to leave your head and land on your lips. Many of the women in my family and I were victims of child abuse. My uncle had a well-hidden mental illness. No one had the courage to shed light on this ugly truth and force it to be addressed. We all just accepted he was sick, and you were lucky if his abuse didn't happen to you. He knew when to prey on us girls, and it worked for those of us who had hardworking parents who were distracted by the demands of making ends meet. I didn't understand what was happening, but I was one of the lucky ones. Even though I was fortunate in the sense of only being molested by him, he fondled me but didn't penetrate. However, I didn't escape from the hatred and the post-child abuse blame issues with trusting men around my girls.

It not only takes a village to raise a child but it also takes a village to protect children. If there's a dark truth being covered up and danced around, I encourage you to be the one to shed light on it so it no longer has the power of darkness to stay alive. This power of darkness is how it survives from generation to generation, and we owe it to our family's legacy. This newfound light can keep issues like this in the past and keep them from repeating. I survived child abuse.

Domestic Violence

Some people believe that everyone has a soul mate. People sometimes call it the person God wants you to be with. This connection between soulmates is based on love and chemistry. I think it takes both. Love alone will take you far, but the chemistry keeps you going. Love feels like butterflies when someone whispers your name, or you get a soft kiss on your collar bone. Chemistry feels like you can have a conversation across a room filled with people without saying one word. The exchange takes place in the eyes and body language. Chemistry is balancing each other's strengths and weaknesses. Each day counts, and there's an appreciation for anticipating each other's needs.

When you get married, you believe it will last forever. You should anyway; otherwise, why are you getting married? Getting married to your childhood sweetheart is a dream for many people. My boyfriend and father of my four children became my husband, and we were unbreakable. There was only one problem: we changed as we grew older. Life changes you. Pain changes you. Eventually, the infidelity, bad decisions, immaturity, addiction, and domestic violence took a toll on us. Our marriage went from being on cloud nine to being on cloud negative ninety-nine. I won't spend much time here, but I will say we no longer brought out the best in each other. We were starting to bring out the worst in each other.

One night in June 2008, I was wearing a t-shirt and panties, positioned on all fours on top of my bed with the barrel of an AK47 to the back of my head. All I could see were visions of what the wall would look like with my splattered brain matter decorating it as he pressed the hard, cold steel against the back of my skull. I closed my eyes, prepared to be snatched out of this world, hoping I wouldn't feel any pain while praying the entire time. As I was praying to God, I heard the click of the trigger. The gun did not fire. My eyes opened. My heart was beating out of my chest. I was still alive on my bed. I ran out the front door, never looking back. That night, I chose to run out of my house in fear of my life, leaving my children behind. It was the moment I knew I could no longer be his wife.

Your husband is supposed to be your protector, not your enemy or competitor. I was most upset that I left my children in the house as I ran barefoot on rocks and grass through yards with barking dogs (I'm scared of dogs). Every mother wants to make their kids feel safe and protect them at all costs. A mother duck will go against a cobra snake without hesitation to save her babies. It's like all mothers get a superpower from God when we need to protect our children. And it's not just about our kids. We see our kids in other kids who are facing danger. It's the universal mother power. So, if every mother is supposed to protect her child even if her own death could be the result, why did I leave my children behind? That was the point of no return for me.

This event happened while I was at the top of my career and pursuing my dream of writing a book—my first attempt. I didn't see this coming, and I wasn't equipped with the tools to recover. It was just too hard. The pain mixed with unforgiveness was a heavy load to carry. Those life lessons we learned together made me who I am today. In 2012, the divorce was finalized.

After the divorce, I had to work on me. It was difficult to enjoy life at the beginning. I was living, but I wasn't *alive*. Nothing was wrong, but something *wasn't right*. I had support from family and friends, but I felt fragile. On the surface, I was a *superwoman* living the dream, but under the surface, I was a constant avalanche of emotions and worry. I had to find a way to pick up the pieces.

I became more of a workaholic (like I was becoming my mother). I traveled every chance that I could. There was a sense of calmness when I didn't have to deal with my reality. Even though it was a toxic marriage, I still felt loss with my divorce: loss of the companionship and who I had identified with since the age of fourteen.

My friends and I made time to party when we could. Let's face it: you can party hard when you work hard. I met men all of the time. I have never had a problem attracting men, even when wearing a messy ponytail and a jogging suit. Once, someone told me that my confidence attracted men. When I found love again, it blindsided me. My boundaries and walls that kept men out, that protected me, were as flat as a pancake. I was smiling again, but it was a different smile. It was deeper, wider, longer, and shinier. This felt good, but I was still lost, healing, and really didn't know how to love myself again, so how in the heck was I going to entertain a healthy relationship? I came from a line of strong women. I had to remember my name and bloodline.

The first step to surviving my divorce was remembering who I was. When I put myself first, I realized I had purpose and was whole before my marriage. I was enough. Yes, you become one in a union of marriage, but you are whole and complete as a single person. The solitude was necessary for me to heal my wounds and come to terms with unpacking the baggage that was neatly packed and stacked for the next guy to deal with. I focused on my personal and career goals.

The next step was drilling down to my why. This was very emotional for me because my why is my children. My children having more options and being able to stand on their own two feet when I'm dead and gone was the only thing that kept me going when it would've been easy to give up. When you truly drill down to your why, it can be emotional. You'll learn more about this in the next section.

The last step that helped me survive my divorce was forgiveness. I learned to forgive by understanding that everything that tore us apart was to reveal our testimony. Holding on to unforgiveness is toxic. Who do you need to forgive? I came to realize I could appreciate the pain and disappointment because it taught me how to be resilient and discover my strengths and weaknesses. I survived domestic violence.

Are you in survival mode right now? What have you survived? Can you relate to any of the things I survived? It's called being a human. We have all survived something. But the key to getting past it is knowing you appreciate each and every experience as I stated before: the good, bad, and the messy. We need the bad experiences to develop those weak areas. Also, we need the bad experiences to appreciate the good experiences.

On top of that, God will never give us more than we can bear. I had no idea how I would heal my wounds, but I had faith to trust God and let him use me when I was in low and high places. The key is remembering those low places you have survived and recognizing them going forward, remembering where you come from. Some people may encourage the suppression of those survival moments. I think we should do the opposite. Remember them so that you will be grateful for where you are now, and it will keep you from going back there if possible.

CHAPTER 2

What the S?!

The **S** in survival mode breaks down into five Ss. Let's take a deep dive into the Ss of survival mode. I want to list each one, and then we'll dive deeper. As we navigate through this list, reflect on what's happening in your life. Later on, we will discuss how to address the S. The Ss are the following:

- Success fear
- Stressors
- Shocks
- Strains
- Struggles

Fear of failure is easier to talk about. Fear goes both ways: failure and success. **Success fear** is very common, but most people don't acknowledge it. Because we act based on how we feel, fear will keep us from taking action. You might be asking yourself: *How can fear of success keep you from starting on your* *goals?* Think about how success may change the current state of life for anyone. Success is a change of what we know as comfort, even if it's considered a good change. So, long story short, success will open the doors of the unknown. It can change how people treat us or how we treat others, disrupt our current trust levels, expose us, or even make us vulnerable. However, both are fears of the unknown.

Entrepreneurship is a huge step for someone used to punching a time clock and depending on a corporation to direct what you do and how much you earn. It really takes a fearless person to climb out on a limb and take a leap into the deep, black hole of gaining customers and building relationships. But what if you succeed? Your mindset will elevate, and everything you're comfortable with will change. Fear of success is usually the killer of an entrepreneurial spirit. We'll talk more about how to overcome the fear of success in Part Three. It takes a combination of remembering your why, confidence, and motivation. Don't worry; the deets are coming!

Stressors are the most common thing we deal with. Stressors cause stress. There are three categories of stress we'll address in this chapter: *life stress, job stress,* and *internal stress*. Stressors can happen at any time, and it may be necessary to deal with more than one stressor at a time. For me, I was dealing with life, job, and internal stressors at the same time. Being pregnant at fourteen, unable to legally work, and feeling ashamed became stressors that I had to cope with. Chapter 1 reveals how it unfolded, but I want to dive deeper in stressors so that you can identify your own stressors and learn a strategy to cope and eventually eliminate.

Life stress presents from anything that can consume your energy. It can be related to family, finances, housing, transportation, a health condition, school, friends, or pets. Family conflicts can cause stress to the entire family. When my grandmother was consumed with Alzheimer's and could no longer take care of herself, my family began bickering over who was going to be responsible for certain tasks and where she was going to live. It started with her children but soon trickled down to her grandchildren and leaped up to her sister.

As mothers, we can get stress from our children. They start off being so sweet and adorable. Then, at some point, they turn into little people that tap dance on our nerves. Our children expect us to move mountains, and we really do try to, but when we can't, we stress about it. My kids think I have limitless access to money. I want to be there for them but get stressed when I don't have the cushion in my budget. Over the years, I've noticed dads can have all the excuses in the world, but moms are expected to figure it out. Do you have any life stressors draining your energy?

Financial stress can drive life-changing decisions. Lack of money and resources is a financial stressor. Not knowing when or what you will be able to feed your children is the reality for many people. Providing is a mother's duty, and when she is unable to do so, it becomes a source of stress. A desperate mother is one decision from taking drastic measures to feed her children. Some mothers will resort to committing crimes to secure money, which could lead to risking her freedom. When I moved out during my senior year, I was faced with dilemmas that involved not having enough money to buy infant formula or have enough money to pay my electric bill. I know several people who made decisions to risk their freedom so that they could provide for their children Some of them paid the price of their freedom, which separated them from their children. I am not putting anyone down; I just want to bring light to how financial stress can change lives.

Job stressors are related to your work duties and environment. As a nurse on the front line, I deal with life and death daily and have the responsibility of millions of dollars of medical equipment and medication. That's a breeding ground for job stress. Healthcare is an industry that doesn't allow second chances. You don't get a second chance to get it right. As a waitress, you can mess up on the kind of drink requested, or as a painter, you can paint a room the wrong color and correct those errors with minimal cost and time. However, the wrong medication or removing the wrong limb has very high stakes. When COVID-19 landed on us, we had a new level of job stress as healthcare workers related to environmental safety and infection prevention. We had to figure out how to maintain operations without spreading the sometimes-fatal virus. As an occupational health nurse, it was challenging to get information and give direction to employees to minimize the risk of COVID-19. This pandemic is changing the face of healthcare and adding to the already high job stressors those professionals experience. Seeing the increased death at younger ages, patients dying alone because of visitation restrictions, and limited personal protective equipment were icing on the crumbling cake.

My nursing career started in bliss. I was working at the largest and most prestigious hospital in Tulsa. My husband and I secured an apartment nearby, and life was good. Shortly after I finished my orientation, I started to question if nursing was the right career choice. My responsibility grew from new nurse to charge nurse in no time, and I was taking a team of up to twelve patients at times on the 3–11 p.m. shift (second shift). An eight-hour shift was turning into 10–12-hour shifts. Going to work started to feel like going to a shooting range with a target on my chest. It wasn't safe, and the money wasn't worth it. It was unsafe for a nurse to be responsible for twelve patients in an acute care setting, and it was stressing me to the max. I lasted roughly nine months before I started looking for a new job with a better experience. I eliminated this job stress by changing employers.

As I entered the new hospital to complete an application, a gentleman greeted me and inquired about what I needed help with. I informed him I was looking for a job. He told me to follow him. As we turned several corners and went upstairs, we finally arrived in an office where I was introduced to a man sitting behind a desk. He smiled so brightly at me and asked if I had any experience with housekeeping. I couldn't believe he assumed I was looking for a housekeeping job. I was confused. I wasn't sure if it was because of my age or my race. I quickly informed the man that I was a registered nurse.

This experience brought light to the fact that there aren't many nurses who look like me, and I would need to perform at my best so other nurses who look like me will get a chance. It isn't right, but the next person who looks like us will get a chance based on how we perform.

I wanted a new job on the day shift in the intensive care unit (ICU) and to be responsible for one to three patients instead of twelve patients—I wanted to have a job that would make me feel eager to work and one where I was making a difference. A medical-surgical floor nurse manager in a hospital that was third in hospital market share called me for an interview. I quickly told him I had no desire to work in med/surg; I wanted to work in the ICU. He persuaded me to interview with him. It ended up being the best decision for me. He was the best manager I have experienced to date. He was a leader by example and had a unique way of challenging his team to perform at our best. We developed bonds with each other and became lifetime friends.

I worked with him for years and grew as a charge nurse and later as a nurse manager. I came to know firsthand the challenges that he faced as a nurse manager. I had to juggle making the patient experience, staff experience, and provider experience great. A nurse manager position is very dynamic. I approached that position as if I was a consultant. I looked at the hospital organization as my client and focused on making their customers (patients, providers, and employees) happy by exceeding their expectations. I wanted to anticipate and predict their needs. This approach helped me focus on what my unit needed and helped motivate me to be the best manager possible. I decreased the agency rate and turnover rate and improved the relationships between the nurses/nurse aids, providers/nurses, and between shifts. Being motivated to do well for my customer, the hospital, allowed me to feel like I was contributing on a different level, which equated to being eager to arrive each day with a smile. This is how I approached my current position as well.

It makes a difference when you have a manager who enjoys what they do and helps you grow. It allowed me to understand what I wanted to be for my team when I became the manager. I survived the armpit of bedside nursing as a graduate nurse.

Changing employers may be the best way to deal with job stress in some cases. Some job stress can be addressed by staying with the employer but changing departments or work groups. The main takeaway here is to identify the source of job stress and take action to deal with it or eliminate it.

Internal stressors are those things that cause stress because of who we are and how we react to things. Internal stressors could be anxiety, depression, or even burnout. The best approach to internal stress is the identification of the source and seeking help. Signs and symptoms vary depending on the person, so the key is noting when things change. You may no longer find joy in things that used to make you smile. Depending on the source, you may recognize it, or someone that is close to you may bring it to your attention. The response to internal stress can be as subtle as withdrawal or creating distance. The takeaway here is to get help so you can address it and overcome it.

It takes resilience, self-care, and remembering your why to overcome stressors. There is a chapter dedicated to each skill you will need to live your best life.

Shocks are another common thing that we must deal with. According to Merriam-Webster, "a shock is a sudden or violent mental or emotional disturbance in the equilibrium or permanence of something" (https://www.merriam-webster.com/dictionary/shock). An example of a shock could be a natural disaster or pandemic. Shocks are usually out of our control. The 2007 ice storm of Tulsa, OK, caused everyone to go into survival mode. Electricity was out for up to ten days for some residents. This led to housing, food, and work challenges. As a nurse manager of an acute care unit during the ice storm, I was dealing with staffing shortages because employees couldn't work without daycare. The daycares were closed because they couldn't operate without electricity or heat. It was like the domino effect. The entire hospital was on a caregiver scavenger hunt for resources to care for the patients, and the managers were in the trenches of this shock. It is the same scenario for tornados, earthquakes, and other natural disasters. The natural disaster you deal with depends on your region. Tulsa is prone to tornados, floods, and ice storms.

A more recent shock is the 2020 pandemic. The Coronavirus landed on us and put all of the infrastructures in place to the test. We failed to plan for this type of shock as a country and worldwide. This shock started in China but soon spread to other countries as doctors and nurses scrambled to meet the demand of patients who faced a sudden onset of symptoms and spreading the virus to family and friends. Everyone had to learn and become experts on proper handwashing, wearing a mask, and being socially distant.

Healthcare providers weren't only the heroes but were also victims. Yes, nurses and doctors were dying from the virus as they were forced, in some cases, to provide care without proper personal protective equipment. Before this, I didn't know of any incidents when there weren't enough N-95 masks, isolation gowns, gloves, disinfectant sprays/wipes, face shields, or ventilators. The nursing shortage went from (in my Drake voice) "zero to 100 real quick." Nurses were refusing to work without proper protective equipment. Hospitals had to make some ethical decisions like who was going to get the last ventilator.

You will learn how to master resilience so when a shock lands on you and rocks your whole world and vibe, you can handle it and still be cute. We can't avoid delays on our success journey, but the difference is how long it takes to bounce back. Also, each delay is an opportunity to gain or learn something.

Strains, according to the Oxford Dictionary, "are a severe or excessive demand on the strength, resources, or abilities of someone or something" (https://www.oxfordlearnersdictionary.com). There can be some overlap with strains and stressors. Strains can be related to family and jobs. The constant strain to do more with less spills over in all aspects of life.

There's usually one person in each family who bears the load for the family unit. In most cases, it's a parent or the oldest child. This person must be strong for everyone. They must have the resources to fill the gap for others and are pulled in a million directions more often than anyone else. They're the first person called upon in the face of trouble. This person is usually hanging on by a thread internally, but they usually don't know they're at the top of the survival-mode mountain.

For example, the 2020 pandemic revealed a tremendous amount of strain that existed in homes and jobs. The mandatory isolation and quarantine orders resulted in an increase in domestic violence and child abuse. The financial strain from not being able to work caused evictions and food-supply challenges. The majority of our country was in survival mode and scrambling to do so. The world was forced to go virtual. Many of the lucky ones were able to work from home, or should I say, live at work. An influx of virtual platforms allowed workers to communicate and operate from home. The only problem was it put workers and students in a position of work invading all aspects of their home. Education and livelihood were strained to the max, and even some more strain was spread on top of that. The pandemic added strain to an already strained society.

Struggles are difficult for us. Some examples of struggles that could be an express train to survival mode are procrastination, lack of skills, lack of confidence, and motivation or lack of motivation. Procrastination is a habit that can be stopped. Even though it's a habit, some people take it on as an identity—a procrastinator. Understanding the impact of your struggles is the first step. Procrastination can cause you to stay paralyzed at a point in life even though you want more and desire to act. We will discuss a few strategies to end procrastination in a later chapter.

Struggling with a lack of skill or skillset is another route to survival mode. For example, communication, decision-making, conflict resolution, and leadership skills are all skillsets people struggle with. But the most prevalent is a lack of time management skills. Time management is key to planning and making goals a reality. There are many moving parts of managing everyday life. How you view time is the first step of understanding how you spend your time. Your time belongs to you, but many people do not see it through that lens. People often approach time from a view that it is separate from you. This makes it easy to allow others to use your time for their needs. When you view your time as being owned by you, it's easy to be more mindful of how you use your time and let others control your time. Time is a landmark for determining what is important to you. There's an old saying: You'll know what is important to someone based on what they spend their time and money on. There is a time-inventory exercise in the next chapter to help shed light on your time-management skills.

Lack of confidence is a struggle that you can overcome with intention. Confidence is all about how you feel. It's important in some cases, and it is okay not to be confident in other cases. If you're embarking on a new journey with no experience, it's totally fine to feel a lack of confidence. You'll get more confidence with more exposure and experience. The difference is when you should have confidence, but you don't. Self-sabotaging thoughts—something we all deal with—can affect your confidence, regardless of whether you're a novice or expert in a certain field. The only thing that changes with experience is how fast you bounce back to an acceptable level of confidence after dealing with self-sabotaging thoughts.

Motivation can be internal or external. I'm going to focus on internal motivation in the next chapter, which will include an exercise to expose internal motivation. When you know what motivates you, you will do things when you don't want to. Also, when your motivation is bigger than you, you won't let anything stop you. Each journey you start will come with challenges, but those won't stop you when you're motivated internally. Challenges actually become a source of motivation.

Self-care and confidence help to manage struggles. Struggles change as we progress on our success journey. In many cases, as you solve a struggle, another one develops. That's just a heads up that struggles will come and go but no worries; you will be ready.

PART 2
Self-Awareness

One of my favorite quotes by Steve Jobs is, "Don't let the noise of others' opinions drown out your own inner voice."[1] It's easy to drown in a sea of information and beliefs. I challenge you to block out the noise and explore a deeper level of yourself. Self-awareness is key to crushing your goals. As you read Part 2, stay true to the process and to yourself. Sometimes, it requires us to be still and reflect. It may be tempting to skip this part and go straight to skill-building, but please don't. Drill down to the details of who you are. Spoiler alert: You will transform to your best version as you crush your goals.

CHAPTER 3

Who Am I?

Do you know who you are? The top two self-sabotaging thoughts that kill your goals are: *I am not enough* ___, and *I do not have enough* ___. You can fill in the blanks if you have ever felt this way. This chapter is all about self-awareness. Self-awareness is about getting real with yourself. Digging in and leaning into who you are will help you experience a transformation from survival mode to living your best life. I want to tell you right now that you are enough, and you have everything it takes to live your best life. You're the master of your success because no one can be you or do what you can do or add what you can add. You get my point. Cherish the person you are now because I promise you will be a different person after you master your ultimate success. As a matter of fact, you will transform at each step of the process. As you are rejected, accepted, making progress, and sharing your story, you will get more courageous, emotional, determined, and unstoppable.

As I mentioned before, most people fall into two categories: trained to stayers (TTSers) and trained to goers (TTGers). TTSers have perfected the art of being fake and getting run over.

No one can know how they feel inside. There's a need to look like everything is together inside. They have no desire to stand up and stop what is happening. Comfort comes to them from being in the thick of it and having an undercurrent of chaos. The only issue with this mindset and way of thinking is their improvement isn't coming because they aren't confronting or dealing with anything. Have you ever known a person who's in a bad relationship? Okay, that was a rhetorical question. Most of us have been in a bad relationship or witnessed a loved one in the middle of pure hell with a significant other. In many cases, it's so easy to see how bad it is from the outside. The person looking in but not in it will often ask, "Why doesn't she/he leave?" But when a person is in the middle of it, they don't have 20/20 vision. When they finally get fed up and reflect back on the relationship after leaving, they'll usually say that they stayed because it was easier to stay than to leave. It was familiar. It was a known evil. Being comfortable will keep you from moving. TTSers are really strong but just not risk-takers.

TTGers are the opposite. Change is coming. They're not ashamed or fearful of revealing what's happening. It's uncomfortable and almost suffocating for a TTGer to be in denial and avoid the effects of chaos. Being self-aware of what's rippling through your body is the stronger position to keep. It will feel weaker to confront the fears and shame. This weakness is survival mode and a trigger to change it.

I think we can be both TTSers and TTGers. It really depends on the phase of life that you're in. But we have a natural tendency to gravitate to one more than the other. It's what makes us human. Again, we make the decision based on how we feel. Don't worry; as you accomplish more self-awareness, you'll discover what you need to become stronger and your best version.

The focus of this section is to discover more about you. Revealing your true colors is the first step. Make sure you don't skip the exercises to get the full benefit. When you get to the end of this section, you'll be ready to start living your best life. Roll up your sleeves and get ready to put in the work. Your best version of you is the reward. Only you can do you better than anyone else.

Your Why

Your why is unique to you. Self-satisfaction and you are usually at the center of the wrong why. When you're drilling down to your why and unable to get past the superficial layers, it's easy to get stuck on the wrong why. The wrong why will make it easy for you to stop and give up when life gets hard and challenging.

There will be highs and lows on your journey to your best life. When you're dragging yourself through a low point in life, it will be easy to fall into the trap of negative thoughts and lose motivation. This journey requires you to be focused on the end while you're at the beginning and in the middle. While you are in the middle of a low, the first step is to acknowledge it. Then assure yourself it's only temporary. At this point, you can pivot your attention to another positive aspect of life. This shift will allow you to quickly rebound to a higher place of feeling motivated and eager.

Another option while you're experiencing a low is you can actually tackle the source and stick with it until you see things turn around. This is the harder of the two options because it requires you to stay in a less-than-optimal period longer. For example, if you're doing two projects, one is creating an invention, and the other is writing a book. A potential low with an invention is funding for developing the innovative idea to become a reality. If the idea is estimated to cost more than what is budgeted, a low could be that a new source of funding has to be secured. This task will involve being confident enough to ask and accept when you are told no. A low for the second project of writing a book could be the lack of knowledge of how to get a book published. During this low, you will be tasked with finding a resource that can provide the information needed to get a book published and compare the best route to take for you. When it gets difficult to get information and you become unsure which publishing option is best, that could be a true moment of lowness. In the moments of lowness, you have to decide if you will stay focused. This is almost impossible with the wrong why.

The right why is bigger than you. The drill-down exercise will prepare you for the right why. The drill-down is roughly five to six layers of the repeated question why. Start asking yourself why your goals are important to you. Whatever answer you get, ask yourself why again. Then ask yourself why again. Then ask yourself why again. Then ask yourself why again. Now, you have your right why. The format we use to drill down to the right why is:

Why is your goal or vision important to you?
Why?
Why?
Why?
Why?

Remember, the right why is going to be something greater than you, something that reaches beyond your current boundaries. This ultimate why will keep you going when you experience a low. We have an intrinsic factor that pushes us to keep going when our why is not centered around the self. It can be hard to understand at times, but we're not eager to disappoint others as fast as we will disappoint ourselves. When you don't want to do what you need to do, you have to be able to draw on something bigger than you for motivation. It's easier to let yourself down than someone else or some higher power. You will be able to stay motivated and eager to crush your goals and become your best version.

I warned you that this would be hard work, but it will be worth it. It's your turn to complete this exercise. Hopefully, you'll learn what's driving you to push through the defensive line on the one-yard line with a pack of players on your back as you keep forcing one foot in front of the other. Share your goal with your family and write it down. Then put it in a place where you'll see it each day.

What's Important to You?

How you spend your time is an indication of what is important to you. Where is your time going? Do you know? The time-inventory exercise is a journaling exercise that will help you shed light on where you're spending your time. It involves a week of tracking tasks and relating them to a goal or hobby. I hear people respond to that question with "there isn't enough time," or they "need more time to get things done." Since no one can add more hours to a day or stop time, we have to manage our time wisely and make sure it aligns with who we are and our goals.

What you spend money on is also an indication of what's important to you. If you were to create a journal to track what you buy for a week, it would allow you to look at what you spend money on. This isn't an easy task because you'll have to keep track of each transaction: credit and cash purchases. One approach could be to make sure you get a receipt and journal all of the receipts at the end of each day. Hopefully, you will find you're spending your money on things that are important to you. If you find you're spending your money on things that aren't important, this will be a wake-up call to make adjustments. Either way, it will be beneficial in shedding light on what's important to you.

Your Attitude

Your attitude is always showing. It's in your facial expression, eyes, body language, breathing pattern, movement, and voice. When someone sees you, they instantly form a conclusion based on what they see. If you're smiling and making eye contact, they may conclude that you have a good attitude, which can be interpreted as being approachable.

Your attitude reflects your energy and feelings. If you're aware of this, it may be easier to focus on positive energy, leading to positive feelings. People feed off your energy. When someone sees you smiling, they automatically start to feel like smiling and connecting with a memory that created happiness for them.

Smiles are contagious. When you are stressed and frustrated, your attitude could be withdrawn or brusque. This type of attitude will make people avoid you or possibly inquire about what is or has happened to you. Most people want to help fix whatever caused your stress or frustration. Are you starting to get it? People see your attitude because it is always showing: good, bad, or ugly. Most people want to be viewed as having a good attitude. Even when you are having a bad day or unable to focus on positivity, putting a smile on your face will prevent people from thinking you need to adjust your attitude.

We have to learn how to change our attitudes. When you acknowledge what you are feeling and transition that to a positive outcome or your why, it can be easier to change your attitude. If you decide that you want your attitude to lift up people around you, you'll find yourself intentionally smiling and being courteous while speaking with people. Before you can feed anyone else, you need to be full. You can't feed anyone when you're on empty.

Now that you know your attitude is always showing, it should be a priority to make sure your attitude has a positive impact on the people you're around. Keep in mind that you don't have to be interacting with another person for your attitude to influence them. They may see you walking into the convenience store and be influenced by your attitude.

Your Needs

Maslow's Hierarchy of needs could be used as a guide of how our needs are prioritized and met.[2]

Maslow's Hierarchy of Needs

01 *Physiological needs*

Air, water, food, shelter, sleep, clothing, reproduction

02 *Safety needs*

Personal security, employment, resources, health, property

03 *Love and belonging*

Friendship, intimacy, family, sense of connection

04 *Esteem*

Respect, self-esteem, status, recognition, strength, freedom

05 *Self-actualization*

Desire to become the most that one can be

Maslow's hierarchy of needs, depicted in the illustration above, shows the summary of how we meet our needs. At the bottom, you have physiological needs, and at the top, you have self-actualization. Maslow explained through his work that you can't achieve esteem until you've met your physiological, safety, and love/belonging needs. If you think about it, this is true for most of us. We can't perform well at work and be productive employees if we are starving. According to Maslow, we should all have a goal to achieve self-actualization, but only after all other needs are met. I won't get into the weeds of this, but I had to share the work of Maslow so that it was clear that there is a method to the madness and chaos of fulfilling needs.

When I was twenty-five years old, I purchased my first home. I didn't have enough furniture to put in the house. My living room only had a couch, and it didn't belong to me. I was just holding it for my uncle. Some people had a lot to say about my empty house. At first, it bothered me, but I knew I had to start with securing my home—furnishing it would come later. I responded to my critics with "at least I own a home." In many cases, the person with so much to say didn't own a home. In addition to my lack of furnishings, my car wasn't reliable. Every time I finished a twelve-hour shift, I needed a jump. It was embarrassing. But I had a grasp on my priorities at that time. So, I worked to finance a reliable car. It felt so good to come out to my car after work and know that it was going to start without a jump. Next, I decided to furnish one room at a time. I wasn't in a rush. I would get antsy and come very close to purchasing furniture on credit, especially after visiting someone with a fully furnished home. Each time, my gut would stop me and remind me that I needed to stick to the plan. It was the best thing for me. Think about it, I bet you know someone who bought a brand-new car for social status reasons, but they're sleeping on their friend's couch. Some people just don't know how to prioritize their needs. Take a few moments to review the Maslow illustration and evaluate how you prioritize your needs.

Vital Needs

Everyone has vital, needs and they're a form of self-care. There's no right or wrong vital need. It's very easy to lose focus of our vital needs. We're often in a constant tug of war between self-care and serving our family, friends, and work. There is a thin line between burnout and balance. We have to be intentional to ensure we meet our vital needs. I will go through a list of the twenty-five vital needs and describe each one. I recommend that you choose seven of them and start making time daily to take part in a vital need.

List of Vital Needs

- Personal time: a need for time that focuses on you and what you want to do
- Giving to others/volunteering: a need for giving time or donating items or money to others
- Recognition for an achievement: a need for being acknowledged for an accomplishment
- Movement: a need to be mobile or moving
- Sleep: a need to rest
- Approval or acceptance: a need to feel approved or accepted
- Order and closure: a need for feeling organized and no loose ends
- Time alone: a need for solitude
- Territory (like a man cave or she shed): a need for something to belong to you
- Financial security: a need to feel an abundance of financial resources
- Being with people: a need to be around others

- Anticipation: a need to feel like something's getting ready to happen
- Competition: a need to compete
- Learning new things: a need to learn or be exposed to new things
- Listening to music: a need for music
- Touch: a need to be touched or close to someone
- Having a project: a need to be working on a project
- Variety of experiences (doing new things): a need for new experiences
- Structured time (routine): a need for a schedule
- Unstructured time (no set routine): a need to have freedom of time
- One-on-one attention: a need for another person to focus on you
- Group relationships: a need to be part of a group
- Empathy: a need to empathize with others
- Humor: a need to laugh
- Spirituality: a need to connect with a higher power

Take the time to study this list and explore how you feel about each vital need. Which vital needs are important to you? Rank your top seven vital needs and start making time for them. Making time for them means you'll be more intentional about creating a work-life balance with self-care.

Vital needs contribute to how we feel. Since most of us make decisions based on feelings, when you meet your vital needs, you have a different response to stressors and triggers. You'll make better decisions and be more engaged. This means that we should be mindful of how we're feeling while we are making decisions.

It might be surprising to realize how you're already meeting some of your vital needs daily. Here's an example: there was a nurse who loved her two-hour commute to work. After her shift, it was her alone time before she arrived home to her family. She was able to unwind from work and just be alone with her thoughts. One day, she was sharing she has a two-hour commute with a coworker, and the co-worker said they could never have a commute that long. These two nurses have different vital needs. Vital needs are not right or wrong for anyone.

Implementing vital needs should be subtle. After determining your top seven vital needs, select three you can start during the first week. (Hint: it's easy to implement small things.) Then, each month, add another vital need until you have implemented all seven. Don't make it hard. Keep it simple and easy. You'll see a difference in how you approach things and respond to situations when you meet your vital needs. Meeting your vital needs fills you up. Being full and balanced will help you be more open and a source of food for the people around you. This means you'll be able to give your energy and full engagement to others. All of this will make more sense in Chapter 10 when we discuss how you can be an inspiration to others when achieving success.

CHAPTER 4

Visions and Goals: Personal and Professional

A vision is simply what you want to be or become. Everyone should have visions and goals. When you have a vision of what you want to become or a goal you're striving for, each day is intentional and purposeful.

I will be breaking down how you should be formulating your visions and goals. Notice that I will be showing you more than one vision and goal. This will allow you to plan for the different levels of life. It's better to break down your vision in three phases for each aspect of your life: personal and professional or business. After speaking with multiple clients, I was amazed by how many people struggle to look at life beyond a year. It can be a difficult task but gets better with practice.

Our purpose and vision come from God. Only God can give those to you. I cringe when I see people selling purpose and vision. It can't come from a person. If someone falls for the idea of getting purpose or vision from someone else, it won't be from God and, therefore, won't be successful. It's easy to get impatient when you want to see results quickly, but I urge you to be patient because everything happens when it's supposed to. Our timing doesn't matter, only God's timing. Keep in mind we still have to set dates with our goals and visions, but we can't get discouraged when the timeline we set isn't met. Just stay faithful to your goals. Keep preparing so you'll be ready when the opportunity falls in your lap. Your faithfulness will pay off. We have a deep understanding that God's Will *will* be done, and He is always on time.

This process starts with taking a moment in solitude to envision what God wants in your personal life, professional life, and business in one year, five years. Ultimately, you'll reach the "Momma, I made it!" level. One year is a short amount of time. The short time-period vision will be a check point for your five-year vision and will feed into that five-year vision.

The ultimate vision will be the point in your life where you have accomplished the highest level of success, abundance, and freedom. That's when you'll be able to tell your momma you made it. At that moment, what will you be doing? It takes practice to envision the details of what you'll see and be doing. After you can visualize it, write it down or put it where it will be visible.

Now, you can start the vision exercise. In this exercise, imagine what you want to be doing in one year, five years, and "Momma, I made it." Keep in mind that God doesn't provide you with a vision without provision. He will make a way for you, and His Will will be done.

Here's an example of a "Momma, I made it!" business vision:

I hear water crashing on the sand/rocks and feel a breeze brushing over my face. My eyes open to soft sunlight shining through fluffy clouds and landing on the waves. My husband's smile greets me as I roll over. I walk over to the table to scrambled eggs with cheese, turkey sausage, and crispy French toast. I glance over my speaking notes as I enjoy my breakfast and OJ. As usual, butterflies are starting to flutter in the pit of my gut before I speak. I hear my grandkids at the door. The oldest granddaughter bluntly asks, "Are you ready, Jah Jah?" My reply makes her growl with frustration.

Soon, I am dressed and headed to the auditorium. 80,000 of my perfect customers fill the auditorium, and I can't wait to give them everything that I have. This event is my fifth speaking engagement on this book tour. I have five more engagements, and then I'll be able to start on my next book. As I'm being introduced, I'm praying backstage. I know I'm in this very moment for a reason, and I want God to use me.

I catch a flight to New York immediately after this. I will be speaking on Broadway. I love working and traveling the world with my husband and kids when it works out. I have abundance and freedom. I end the day by answering emails while sipping tea and thanking God for his vision, faith, and provision.

Now, it is your turn to be specific and detailed about what you want to see in your visions. Write it down below. Say it out loud. Your words have power. Share this with your accountability partner.

Vision: One Year
Personal Vision
Professional Vision
Business Vision
Vision: Five Year
Personal Vision
Professional Vision
Business Vision
Vision: Momma, I Made It!
Personal Vision
Professional Vision
Business Vision

Vision Boards

Our visions have to be visible. One way that has gained popularity is creating a vision board. Use pictures and words you want to identify with to create your vision board. Try to keep it simple so it won't be a distraction. Usually, a vision board has to be updated annually. It can be a fun group activity or a solo activity. Place the vision board in a location where you'll be able to view it daily as a reminder of what will be happening one day.

If you need guidance or inspiration for your vision board, there are tons of examples on the internet and YouTube. I have a YouTube video on making a vision board on my channel, Jamesha Ross, RN. Please feel free to use it as a guide if this is your first time creating a vision board. A step further could include hosting a vision board party for New Year's Eve.

Goals

Goals are things that you want to achieve or obtain. You should always have a goal you're striving to reach. When you crush your goals, make new ones. Goals motivate you and require your attention daily. Being obsessed with your goals is a good thing and will be instrumental in making them a reality.

I have an annual event around Thanksgiving called Goals and Chill. This is a virtual event to help nurture goals as the year is winding down to have a strong finish. Start thinking outside the box on how to approach your goals.

Long Term vs. Short Term

Your goals should be a combination of long term and short term. A long-term goal is usually something that will take four to five years to accomplish. As a rule, one of your long-term goals should be so big it scares you. It needs to make you uncomfortable in a challenging way.

A short-term goal usually takes less than a year to accomplish. Your goals should be in alignment with your vision. Your vision is what you are or want to become. Usually, you can break down your long-term goal into several short-term goals. It's a good idea to limit your long-term goals to three. This will keep you from getting overwhelmed. When you start to feel overwhelmed, it can lead to you feeling stuck, which isn't good for your motivation. Remember, what is meant for you cannot be taken away, and what isn't meant for you, you don't want.

SMARTish

Your goals should be SMART, the acronym for formulating goals:

- **Specific**—Your goal should be detailed enough to keep you on the right track. If you plan to get a degree, your goal should be specific to the discipline and what kind of degree. An example would be a bachelor's degree in the science of nursing.

- **Measurable**—Your goal should include a factor that will be easy to determine whether it was achieved or not. For example, the measurement will be graduation.

- **Achievable**—Your goal should be realistic. For example, you should choose a nursing program that will work for your life situation.

- **Relevant**—Your goals should be aligned with your vision, personal or professional. For example, a nursing degree is relevant to becoming a healthcare provider.

- **Time Bound**—Your goal should have a time limit or a due date. For example, I will complete my degree by May of 2024.

Once you have your goals listed, they need to be prioritized. Solely base your prioritization on what makes sense for you.

Some people prioritize their goals based on how fast they will see results, while others prioritize based on the financial impact of the goals.

One example is a goal of eliminating bad debt (debt that doesn't generate income for you). An approach could be paying off your credit cards. There are two methods you could use in the scenario: the snowball or the avalanche method. Both methods will accomplish the goal, but there are different reasons for using the methods. If you're a person who needs instant gratification, you'll be motivated by the snowball method by paying the smaller balances first; it'll feel like you're making progress. If you don't need instant gratification, you'll be motivated by the savings on paid interest with the avalanche method. There's no right way or wrong way. It's very important to focus on what is going to be more helpful for you.

Now that you've finalized and prioritized the goals, the individual tasks for each goal need to be listed in order, if indicated. After you list all the tasks, you'll need to schedule them on your calendar. The calendar can be digital or paper. By adding the tasks to your calendar schedule, you can create reminders. They will prevent you from getting busy and overlooking the tasks that need to be accomplished and keep you on track to meet your date of completion target. The other benefit of scheduling your task is it will be a way to track progress. You'll be able to celebrate progress, big and small. Progress should be a reason to celebrate.

Don't get delayed on tasks because you're trying to make each task perfect. This idea of perfection will be an instant motivation drain because it will never be perfect. If you're waiting for perfect timing or situation, it will be an instant drain of your motivation.

The last point to make on this topic is to make sure you believe in your vision or goal so much that you're obsessed with it. This hyper-focus will be a source of motivation and will keep you on target for crushing your goals. You have to think about it every day and do something every day or every other day: journaling about the goal, talking about it, and visualizing it. Some people benefit by creating a vision board or a meme on the phone. Make sure you place a physical reminder where you have to see it daily.

Goal Categories

I like to focus on four goal categories: *physical, financial, time,* and *social*. Balance is important when you weave resilience into each aspect of goals. Focusing intensely on one category but neglecting another category isn't the best approach. The following is an unprioritized description of the four goal categories.

Physical Goals—any goals that focus on your physical being. Most people focus on health and activity desires. Some examples include weight, chronic conditions, exercise patterns, eating patterns, or self-image.

Financial Goals—any goals that address your financial status. You can approach finances in many ways, including budget, credit, savings, streams of income, net worth, filling the gap with donations, and investment.

Time Goals—any goals that relate to how you manage your time. Time is related to freedom, knowledge, and abundance.

Social Goals—goals that relate to how you interact with others, including relationships, influence, and status.

We will go into more detail on these categories later in the Resilience chapter, but I wanted to introduce you to what we will be working on.

PART 3
Crushing It

As you navigate through Part 3, be open-minded to all of the skills you will build. Each skill will help you crush your goals and lead to becoming your best version that will achieve the highest level of success.

Once, I attended an event for Oklahoma's Speakers Association. Rory Vaden, the guest speaker, shared his quote: "Success is never owned. It is only rented, and the rent is due every day." (speech, Tulsa, OK, February 23, 2012)[4] I love this quote. It describes what will be required each day. We have to pay success rent each day. Sometimes the rent is small, and sometimes it's large. Just pay it or, in other words, just do what needs to be done. Goal crushers, roll up your sleeves even more because it's time to work. Spoiler alert: you'll never run out of success rent; you are enough.

CHAPTER 5

Busy Being Busy

As you read this chapter, focus on how you view time management, accountability, and intention. Each topic is broken down for you to challenge your current status and how you can make improvements in these areas. I share what has helped me and will hopefully help you too.

Time Management

Time. Some people wish they had more of it. I say, let's be grateful for the time we have and make the most of it. We own our time and should use it how we want. When you fill your time with tasks, you are busy. I used to be busy from sunup to sundown. Some of the tasks were for my children and me, while others were for other people. When the day is done, do you feel like you made any progress? Did you accomplish anything, or were you just busy being busy?

Accomplished should be how you feel when the day is over. If you're reviewing what you did for the day and can't pinpoint an accomplishment, that might be a sign of being busy doing the wrong things. How do you measure accomplishment? I used to measure accomplishments by what I crossed off my to-do list, the one I wrote every morning. As the day went on, I would cross off my tasks. At the end of the day, if there was something left on the list, I would add it to the next day's to-do list. Now, I use the calendar on my phone. I schedule my tasks and use the reminder feature to make sure I don't overlook any tasks. In addition, I create my tasks weekly. If there's a task I need to add within a day's notice, it's added the night before.

If you're a person who gets easily distracted when you pick up your phone, you may want to stick to managing your time in a physical planner. Planners do work and will prevent you from being distracted by the many functions of your phone. When scheduling my tasks now, the most important consideration I base it on is traction. Which tasks are going to create traction for me or help me get to the next level? A burst of energy goes through my gut when I hit the next level or gain traction. This energy fuels the momentum for my goals. Other people will see it and want to know what that energy is about.

Talking about your traction is powerful because our words have power. I gained traction with one of my mobile apps after an interview with a local news channel. It was exposure for the application, and my app users increased dramatically after viewers were directed to my website. I was able to gain traction with a gain of 400 users in less than a week of the interview airing. I shared the interview and results on my social media. I shared the app with anyone that would listen.

As I was saying, your time is yours. Review what you're doing and determine if you're spending your time on your tasks or what other people have asked you to do. If you find you're wasting your time doing a lot of things for others, you may need to learn how to protect your time. There is a fine line between being a yes woman/man and being a no woman/man. My rule of thumb is this: I only say yes to what I truly want to do. That's a boundary. When you define your boundaries, stick to them. Don't let people rob you of your time. Some people have mastered how to use your time and make their problems your problems.

One way to prevent this is by saying no. Saying no is a fine art. You don't need to explain why you are saying no, but if you do, make sure you tell the truth. Don't sugar coat it; keep it raw and uncut. You'll avoid confusion if you do. For example, some people say no and then follow it with "I don't have time." Saying, "I don't have time" leaves room for the person to ask you again on another day. When you follow no with "I don't want to do that," it makes it very clear you won't be doing it that day or any other time in the future. This should prevent you from getting the request at a later time.

Time is something you can't get back. We can't go back in time and redo things or get any wasted time back. As a college student, have you ever been asked to accompany a friend to an event? Did you go instead of studying? Were you thinking about what you needed to study instead of having a good time at the party? You went against your plans for your time for someone else's feelings.

Reflecting on this and other similar scenarios will make you understand you really have to be mindful of how you allow your time to be spent. I have started asking myself, *Is there anything I should be doing right now?* Sometimes, I double-check my calendar and even look ahead a day to see if I can do something today instead of tomorrow. Be able to live with and be happy with your time choices. Make every effort to use your time in alignment with your goals. The people around you should have a deep respect for your dedication and focus and not take it personally when you use your time the way you see fit.

Accountability

Accountability is crucial to staying on target. Everyone needs an accountability partner. You could even take it up a notch and get an accountability squad, which could include your closest friends, your children, or selective family members. When you get an accountability partner or squad, you'll need to be in both roles: the person being held accountable and the person ensuring accountability. One of the ways to ensure tasks are completed is to ask for proof. You and your accountability partner can decide if you want daily or weekly check-ins. The method of checking in can be a simple text or phone call. Whatever you agree upon, make sure that you stick to it so it'll be effective in crushing your goals.

Just start and get your first day under your belt or get your first version done. The first time you do something will suck. Just start because there won't be a time when everything will be perfect. You have to come to grips with the fact that now is the perfect time. Make the decision if today will be day one or hopes for one day. Just start now.

I have an accountability group with my sister and children. We are in different states, but we text each other and request proof. Sometimes, it can get a little tense, but it's beneficial to have an accountability squad that keeps it real with you. Having a reliable squad will promote growth and motivation. We motivate each other to think outside our comfort zone and stretch our visions and goals. It's easy to give each other words of encouragement and much harder to call someone out. It takes a level of care to call someone out on not completing goal-oriented tasks. For example, my sister sends me a text message to ensure that I have completed my cardio exercises. Let me warn you, though. No one will hold you accountable like your children. I don't care what age they are. As a child, they will tell you in a heartbeat, "No, Momma, you said we were going to ride our bikes today." As an adult, they will text you in a heartbeat, "Send me a picture of your salad." I think it's natural for them to hold us accountable.

As you're on your journey to the next chapter of your best life, things will pull you in a million directions. You should be obsessed with your goals, and every day should be dedicated to doing something for your goals. Strategic prioritizing will be your bestie and your best tool for crushing your goals.

Intention

Starting your day with intention keeps you on task and engaged. Without intention, you could spend your day reacting to people and things. It's similar to watching *The Walking Dead*: when the walkers respond to seeing a person or hearing a sound, their path changes. We don't want to spend our day on aimless activity that amounts to nothing, allowing other people to define our daily activities without having intentional actions. We want to feel accomplished and like we're making progress toward living our best life and crushing goals.

As a mom, wife, nursepreneur, inventor, success coach, friend, sister, cousin, daughter, and author, I have mastered the subtle art of living my best life. I have people who love me, hate me, envy me, push me, doubt me, and are inspired by me. You do too. If you think about it, you'll start to identify what names belong to each description.

It's important to understand it takes all kinds of people to make the world go round. That means that each type of person is necessary and has a purpose in your life or season. Just remember to trust a person for who they are. It takes too much of your energy not to.

But this section is about trusting who you are. After completing each task, you should have a better idea about who you are at this moment. Your core won't change, but how you respond to people, situations, and all of the above will change as you progress on your journey to living your best life.

Take note of the experience at each step of your journey. Don't skip anything because you're supposed to gain or lose something with progress. If you skip a step, you may miss out on the opportunity for growth. Let's just say that the setbacks are setups in most cases. You may be disappointed something didn't go as planned. Little did you know, though, that setback was an opportunity to regroup or continue to build your credit so you can finance more with a better rate.

Once, I was upset because I didn't get selected for a position. A few months later, another opportunity opened up, and I was selected. My employer created that position to help Oklahoma merge with Illinois, New Mexico, and Texas. It required travel and sharpened my skill set on many different levels. I loved the growth and the networking. I was very fortunate to be the first person in that role and have a new mentor in my supervisor. After being selected, I understood why I wasn't chosen for the first position and was even more thankful to God for leading my footsteps. I encourage you to remember that everything happens when it is supposed to and that it's God's timing.

CHAPTER 6

Self-Care Matters

Caring for yourself isn't selfish. It breaks down to simply doing something for you or your betterment. The best approach to balance life, job, and internal stressors along with struggles is self-care. There's a constant balancing act between your self-care and everything else. Once you start putting yourself first, you'll be in a better position to crush your goals and allow yourself to live your best life. Just dipping your toe into self-care will make you want to dive in headfirst. It takes daily effort, but a combination of small tasks and lifestyle changes are necessary in some cases. Self-care tasks and vital needs can overlap. Review the vital needs list to see what you can add to your self-care list. This chapter focuses on techniques and actual things that you can start practicing today.

Meaningful Morning

My eyes pop open as my alarm blasts into my ears and vibrates on the nightstand. I roll to my left to kiss my husband and interlace my fingers with his fingers. "Our Father God, we come to you in prayer . . ." is whispered with our eyes closed and heads relaxed. We start each morning with prayer. It's our quiet time with God.

How you start your morning sets the tone for the rest of the day. Your morning should be meaningful. I have shared my morning routine with many of my students. Meaningful mornings should be time spent well. Some of the things that have helped me are prayer, meditation, *The 5 Second Rule* by Mel Robbins, reading, journaling, listening to an audiobook, listening to music, and exercise. Your morning time is the perfect time to tend to some of your vital needs. When your morning is meaningful, you can be intentional and fully engaged in your daily tasks. Then it won't be easy for stressors or struggles to interfere and throw you off.

Protect Your Energy

My energy is what I want to carry internally, and it naturally shows with my actions and my attitude. I strive for positive energy, but it is a constant choice—my choice. I choose to keep my energy and protect it from negativity. If you allow someone or something to change your energy, you give them your God-given power. I don't know about you, but I don't want anyone to have the ability to control my energy and feelings.

One of the things that keeps me from giving up my energy is knowing other people can't make their problems my problem. I can choose to assist and listen, but I don't have to take on the burden. If I decide to go a step further to solve a problem, I won't do it with the intention of owning the problem. This is a protection technique.

Another technique is recognizing when a person is draining your energy or is poisonous to your energy. Energy drainage can come in many forms. A common way for someone to drain your energy is by constantly needing validation from you. A person may be poisonous to your energy if they always call you to gossip and talk negatively about other people. You may not feel it during the call, but you often don't feel good after you hang up. Those people leave you with less instead of filling you up. Toxic people may be around you, trying to kill your dreams and poison your goals. When you recognize who these people are in your life, be mindful of what you share with them. Don't give them any fuel to help spread the fire that's coming back to burn you. Sometimes, it's immediate, while other times, it may take a while. Rest assured that it'll show up red hot one day. Have you ever shared an idea with a toxic person? It may go a little like this after you've exposed your goal of starting a business. A typical toxic response could be "how are you going to get customers?" or "are you going to start a business and work full time?" Who comes to mind? Be honest with yourself. Stop telling that person about your goals.

Likewise, you have to make sure you're not draining the people around you. Don't be that friend who's always taking and never giving. Add value to each relationship you are blessed with. Are you letting people borrow your talents when you can? Are you interacting with people from a good place? I have family members who complain about how much they do for others and find a way to bring it up later when they want something in return. It makes me feel when they offer to help me, there's a hidden agenda. Which, in turn, drains me because I'm trying to figure out my problem. So, don't be that person who lurks around with hidden agendas and drains everyone around you. There will be an exchange in many cases, but a good practice is to give more than you take. With that in mind, balance how you navigate and foster relationships.

Gratitude

Self-care includes practicing gratitude. We live in a world that makes it acceptable to complain and focus on the negative instead of being grateful for what's working in our favor. The enemy to gratitude is entitlement. When we allow entitlement to creep into our thoughts, it kills our sense of gratitude. Even when something isn't happening the way we want it to, there are still many things to be grateful for. It's like when you have a flat tire on the way to work. It can make you late to work and miss an important meeting. That can be disappointing. But being grateful that you didn't have a wreck when the tire went flat is practicing gratitude. It's like a light switch to keep your mood in good standing. Use it frequently.

The first person I usually share things with is one of my daughters. She's my biggest fan and supporter. When I published my first ebook, she was the first person to purchase one. Not only did she purchase one, but she bought five. She's my joy. I can share anything with her, and she'll help me figure out how I can get it done with encouragement and accountability. I make sure I nurture her and applaud her because I'm grateful for her love and support. Who's your biggest fan?

Faith

Faith means believing in something you can't see. Have faith in your best version of yourself. Have faith in your visions and goals. Have faith in yourself. Your daily tasks and intention should be faithful to you. The drive and focus that comes with faithfulness is hard to explain. Self-care keeps you faithful to yourself and God. We have to be dedicated to self-care to be in the proper condition and ready for God to use us. God will use us when we're not qualified. He will close the gap to get us to the next level in life. Our faith has to be constant and unwavering. For example, if we have committed to doing cardio three times per week, we will need to fall on our faith to make sure that it happens.

I could go on and on about faith. I love the way Pastor Michael Todd breaks it down. He's the lead pastor at Transformation Church in Tulsa. His book, *Crazy Faith*, is amazing and will be an awesome resource for a deeper dive into faith. I love his quote: "It's only crazy until it happens."[3] That sums up everything. We don't realize that there are no limits on our faith, but we like to put a cap on our faith. Why do we do that? God doesn't. Keeping faith in your goals and aligning them with your purpose is a method of self-care. It fulfills us to hope for what could be and hold on to it. When goal crushing starts with the end in mind, we're more likely to stay faithful until the end. Remember that your purpose comes from God. You only have to pay attention to what God is doing in and around you.

As nurses, we start planning for our patient's discharge at the time of admission. We communicate the discharge plans with the patient to set the expectation. It's very similar to your efforts toward your goals. Focus on the end result and keep faith as a priority.

CHAPTER 7

Confidence

Confidence, resilience, and motivation all overlap and complement each other for success. They work together within a delicate and complex system like our bodies. Our body is a complex system formed by smaller systems that are intertwined and depend on each other and compensate for each other automatically. This chapter will focus on confidence, which is similar to the skeletal system. The skeletal system is responsible for supporting our body. All of the bones connect and support the entire body. For example, all three of the shoulder bones work together to support weight. This can be a simple task like carrying a purse on your shoulder or supporting your body while doing pushups.

Confidence is in the background supporting everything we do. It's required to start, keep going, and finish all tasks and will help you turn one day into day one. Just start with nothing but confidence—you'll learn as you go. You may not be qualified or have all of the desired training, but if you have confidence in your ability to get things done, you'll complete the first version of whatever it is you're focused on. Remember, there's always room for improvement, and progress is better than perfection.

So, don't get stuck trying to make everything perfect and not make progress.

Our confidence is mostly nonverbal. Our actions tell the story of our confidence. In this chapter, I'll show you some ways to find and improve your level of confidence, which will help resolve success fear.

We should aspire to take our confidence to another level—superwoman confidence. Who's your favorite superhero? My favorite superhero is Superwoman. Actually, I have "Superwoman" tattooed on my right shoulder. She was confident in her strength and power to take down villains, and she saved the world each time. She was ready, ready.

I used to struggle with confidence when I needed to present a topic at work or for any type of public speaking. My inner thoughts would take over and tell me I wasn't good or smart enough to speak. Most of the time, I was in a room with a group of people who didn't look like me and, in some situations, made it intentionally uncomfortable. Their exaggerated body language and brusquely toned rhetorical questions were striving to make me feel inferior. I had to use my superwoman confidence to get through those moments. It's similar to how Beyonce transforms into her alter ego, Sasha. When I'm fully wearing my superwoman confidence, I'm fearless and have the confidence to do what I have been trained to do. As a nurse, I am a licensed resource for a number of topics. Some topics are from my nursing-practice experience, and some are from my passions. We all have an inner force that helps us with confidence. Remember that God has your back—let Him use you.

Remember Who You Are

You're unique and have a unique competitive edge. You're the sum of your experience and opportunities. You can't be anyone else, so embrace the beautiful facts of your being. You can't duplicate the cloth you're cut from. As we grow up, it's easy to look at another person and see things that appeal to you, like their hair or style, and wish you had similarities. But you should always look for what you rock at and know that every improvement you want to address is what someone else is wishing for. That's just how it works. We want what we don't have, and other people want what we have. It takes a great deal of intention to remember who you are. Your energy is going to be different, but you have to show up. You have to show up every day as you are. It's all about you and what you bring to the room, table, or environment.

When you were growing up, did anyone tell you that you could be anything if you put your mind to it? Did someone tell you the sky is the limit? Did anyone encourage you to aim high? You become what you believe you can be. As a child, you knew no limits. After you started listening to what other people said and society told you, you began feeling limited. It seems like everyone is judging you and telling you what you will be, and if you listen, you'll start to believe it. As a pregnant teen at fourteen, people told me I wasn't likely to finish high school, and I'd probably be on welfare the rest of my life. But I had a grandmother I spent a great deal of time with who made sure she told me the truth: my life wasn't over because I was going to be a teen parent. My life was going to be different, maybe even harder, but not over. She had high expectations for me. Because I heard that from her, I had high hopes for myself, and I never let my child hold me back. Actually, she motivated me to work harder and be more determined. I wasn't going to let society put me in a system-limiting box and keep me from reaching my potential. My potential was the greatest level of success, in my opinion, to inspire others to do more. On my journey, people often complimented me because they noticed how I was moving and busting through barriers. It's easy to say what you're going to do, but people pay attention when you show them.

You are amazing and have a mixture of feelings that only you can turn into actions. How you handle situations is amazing, and you always show up with good intentions. You're never afraid to do the right thing. How do you face challenges? You show up with your "A" game when it matters. You're strong too. Strength shows up when you least expect it. Once you have made up your mind you need to do something, you get it done.

You are fearless. Fear leaves, and strength drops down on you to get through defining moments. Moments of truth are unavoidable, and that's how you discover your truths. It often takes one thought to get you on track and focused, remembering who you are. Certain moments can pull you into the spotlight. This spotlight requires you to look at where you are on your journey in a relationship, career, age, or health. This spotlight will show you things you don't see unless a light is shining on it and its intensity is magnified. How many times have you forgotten who you are? What I am asking is if you let the task or the desire overshadow you and your truth. Right before I became a teen mom, I was so wrapped up in making my boyfriend feel my love and was eager to get his love and acceptance back that I let that eagerness to feel loved and part of something take over who I knew myself to be. There is a quote that I love by Jim Rohn: "You're the sum of your closest five friends." Who are you spending your energy with, and what are you feeding your goals?

As I mentioned before, you're the sum of your experiences. Sometimes, we have to be intentional about recalling those moments of discovery. I encourage you to take a moment to list those challenges. This list needs to start with your earliest years and progress to the present time. For example, my challenges in life started with my child abuse in grade school by a family member. Think of this task as listing those moments that cause pain, uncertainty, and even doubt in some cases. Every emotion will show up during a challenge. The only thing that changes as we get better at coping with challenges is the amount of time we spend on each emotion. Some of my more significant experiences progress from child abuse, gang violence, domestic violence, discrimination regarding my race, divorce, and my child's mental crisis. Once you have completed your list, I want you to take a moment to reflect on how you felt during that time of your life and what helped you get through it. I know this will be hard for some of the challenges. It took a long time for me to be able to discuss my domestic-violence experience. Going through this list may take some time, but you need to complete it so you understand how strong you are. You are a survivor.

Humble Brags

Humble brags are your accomplishments. They're things we're able to pat ourselves on the back for doing. It's not about getting a big head or being conceited. It's just simply noting that you did something. What are your humble brags? What have you put energy in to complete? If you put energy into achieving an accomplishment, it had some level of importance to you.

Take a moment to list your accomplishments. Start from grade school and work your way to the current year. Most of us have a difficult time with this task because it feels like bragging. After this list is complete, you can review it and pinpoint why you completed each task. This process will shed light on what was important to you regarding each accomplishment.

When I made my humble-brag list, I discovered it had been so long since I reflected on my accomplishments I'd forgotten about quite a few things, like completing a full marathon with my best friend in the fifth grade. During this exercise, I had a newfound sense of confidence from each task. Looking back over each year with the intention of what I was able to complete made me eager to remember. I was shocked with my list, and I wanted to add more things, as I am an overachiever.

Now, work on your list. Be warned that you may arouse emotions you didn't know existed. Be proud of everything on your list. Again, it's your list, and you gained something from each accomplishment. Each accomplishment contributes to your unique competitive edge. Yes, there may be similarities to how you and someone else may complete a project, but no one will do it exactly like you. Let that sink in.

You'll have many factors impact how you start a business venture and keep it thriving. All these factors make it difficult for business partnerships to prosper. In the beginning, everything is wonderful, and you agree on each decision. But as the business evolves with the changing climate of the market, there may be a difference in agreement for some decisions. For example, one business partner may want to expand services within a location to generate income. The other business partner may want to keep services the same but expand with a new location to generate income. The partner with the most percentage gets to make the final decision. In each partnership, one partner should have more ownership than the other. The percentage breakdown can be 51% to 49%. That's essentially an equal partnership, but one person ultimately has more control over decisions. This will keep the business moving forward and hopefully save the partnership. The point is, no matter how similar people think, each person still wants to nurture their unique competitive edge.

You may want to go into a saturated field. Or perhaps you want to speak on a topic that someone else is covering. Don't worry about what others are doing. The strategy to enter a saturated market is doing something different. It doesn't have to be a huge difference—it can be simple. Think about all of the rental car companies that you can choose to rent from. Now, think about the difference in cars. No, not much of a difference there. Think about which rental car company will bring the car to you. Only one should come to mind. Being the rental car company that will bring you a rental car sets them apart from the other companies located at the airport or other locations.

I consider myself to be a motivational speaker and success coach. There are tons of motivational speakers, but none of those speakers have my experiences to share with the audience. No one can tell my story as I can. Each speaker will tell their stories to relate to the audience and deliver their version of motivational techniques to spark a change in the audience. Just focusing on my approach and not on other people in my line of work helps me stand out. Also, not viewing other motivational speakers as competition but potential partners is key to succeeding. In conclusion, use your accomplishments and your unique experiences as a foundation for your confidence. You did it, and you got this.

Positive Affirmations

Positive affirmations can help you transition to a success mindset. I use positive affirmations to limit the negative thoughts that creep into my head when I feel unappreciated and overworked. Negative thoughts can be self-sabotaging and cause you to doubt your ability. Your brain wants to keep you safe. Lots of science supports your brain doing what it can to keep you at a baseline level with your heart rate, blood pressure, and breathing rate. Every negative thought is your brain trying to keep you safe. This concept means when you get excited about a new business venture, your body starts to react. This reaction includes your heart rate increasing, your blood pressure going up, and your breathing gets faster. Your brain makes a note of this and goes into protection mode. It starts sending negative thoughts to you to sabotage your new business-venture idea. Some examples are *you'll never be able to do this because you don't have any experience*, or *no one will buy anything from you*. These thoughts will keep you from taking action if you're not aware of ways to overcome them. When you stop getting excited, your heart rate, blood pressure, and breathing rate will return to normal.

I said and wrote my positive affirmation. Some people find it helpful to put each confirmation on a sticky note and place the notes on a mirror or a place they won't go unnoticed and can be read often.

Speaking the affirmations, give them power. There's power in spoken words. I made my cellphone wallpaper of a list of positive affirmations. This minor change caused me to read my list each time I picked up my phone or locked my phone. The following is my list of positive affirmations:

- I am beautiful.
- I am smart.
- I am worthy.
- I am not broken.

- I am enough.
- I am determined.
- I am special.
- I am kind.
- I am loving.
- I am living in my purpose.
- I am intelligent.
- I am trying and never giving up.
- I am grateful.
- I am humble.
- I am open.

As you're crushing your goals and becoming your best version, you'll transform as a person. Your thoughts will begin to change as you move forward on your journey and experience more. Before you start and, in the beginning, your thoughts might be similar to *am I enough?*, *do I have enough?*, and *there are so many things in the way*. But as you build confidence and start believing in yourself, your thoughts change to *I am enough, I have what I need, or I'll get it*, and *how can I get these things out of the way so I can finish nursing school with kids?* I can't wait to see your best version. You got this!

CHAPTER 8

Resilience

Regarding the body, resilience is similar to the nervous system. The nervous system is the messenger for the body. Neurons take messages where they need to go throughout our body for action to take place or stop. It's like when you touch a hot stove, the nerves in your finger send a message to your brain that the stove is hot and to move your finger.

Resilience is the communicator of our success. When you face a stressor, shock, or struggle, your brain sends a message to activate the different types of wealth you need to lean on. Some situations only require one kind of wealth, but others are so multifaceted it requires multiple types of wealth to survive, adapt, and thrive.

Resilience is when you bounce back after a stressor, shock, or struggle. Some of us have been thrown under the bus and ran over three times or more. It's truly a miracle to get back to standing on ten toes. Resilience is like being planted. We all know that once a tree is planted and those roots grow, it's near impossible to knock it over.

I defined and explained all five of the Ss in Chapter Three. This chapter is about how you bounce back. It always sounds easier than it is. What makes the bounce back easier for some people and harder for others? Why does it seem like some people are back on track in no time, and others just can't get it right? I'll break it down for you.

Have you ever needed to buy another car, and when you finally decided which car you wanted, the dealership tells you that you weren't approved? You start thinking about how you'll get to work and who can give you rides until you can buy a car. I remember when I was denied a loan on a car because of my income. I had a credit score of 720, but my income wasn't enough to support a car payment and rent. My only option for that car was to get a cosigner. Without a cosigner, my plans had to pivot from my own transportation to sharing cars until I could save enough money to pay cash for a vehicle. Getting a cosigner would be using my social wealth, which includes relationships. I needed a good, strong relationship with a person who had good credit and enough income to get me approved. Sharing cars until I could save money to pay cash was activating my financial wealth. My financial wealth was weak in the debt-to-income area but was stronger in the savings area.

Another example is how I was able to prevent burnout after COVID-19 landed on us in 2020. As I mentioned before, I am a registered nurse who's been practicing in occupational health for the past fourteen years. Occupational health focuses on making sure our patients and workers can work safely and promote health. Our clinic became overwhelmed with calls and visits related to COVID-19. I remember coming in to work with ninety-eight voicemail messages one day. The worst part about it was I knew the calls and visits weren't going to slow down enough for me to listen to the messages and return the calls. The pain point for me was the number of patients who could not get direction quickly. Because workplaces were considered super spreaders, we needed to do everything we could to minimize the risk and keep our patients safe, healthy, and informed. I brainstormed how I could meet the demand of the employees and prevent burnout. I developed a mobile application that would allow the employees to perform self-screenings based on the recommendations of the CDC. After completing the screening, a recommended work status would be immediately available. The app eliminated the wait time for the employee to get directions. In addition, the app allowed the nurse to focus on other things. There were some other advantages, but I was happy with reducing the manual screenings by a nurse.

The stressors in my job activated my time wealth. I was able to use my knowledge to change a manual process into an automated process. Being overwhelmed and overworked was pushing me closer to the flames of burnout. I was able to transform from burnout to being refreshed and energized by innovation. This shift resulted in more freedom.

Let's start diving deeper into wealth. There are four types of wealth to focus on so you can ensure you land on your ten toes. A balance between all four types is necessary for resilience. One type of wealth can't be the focus of all your energy and effort while you neglect the others—it won't be in your favor and won't lead to your resilience. Ultimately, we want to be able to withstand adversity with confidence and grace.

Physical Wealth

Physical wealth focuses on your physical health and state of being. Your physical wealth starts with preventative health milestones. Preventative health involves knowing and meeting the milestones for your age, sex, and race. Risk factors are the basis for milestones.

As a nurse, I'm mindful of my physical wealth. I want to educate people on health topics as indicated, and there is a certain level of trust and confidence when I say that I'm doing what I am teaching. The other types of wealth are dependent on your physical wealth. We'll pull it all together at the end of the chapter, but for now, I want to list some preventative health milestones for myself.

Everyone should have an annual physical exam with lab. The lab test should be the basis for what you need. I recommend you discuss your health milestones with your primary care provider. As a middle-aged, African American woman, in addition to my annual physical exam, I get a yearly mammogram and well-woman check with a pap smear and a colonoscopy every ten years since the age of thirty-five. Be on the lookout for more innovation in this area. Some innovators are developing ways to get a snapshot of your health state and risk based on new things.

Vaccination

Included in preventative health are vaccinations. There's a great deal of controversy right now related to COVID-19 vaccines. I believe vaccines work, but I understand both sides. I think the government has a duty to protect the public's health regarding communicable diseases, and I know some people don't desire to be vaccinated and don't want to be forced by the government to do so. I encourage my patients to make the best decision for themselves and be okay with living with their decision. If you are pro-vaccination, make sure you discuss your options with your primary care provider to ensure you have all of the recommended vaccines.

Dental Care

In addition, your physical wealth will include your dental health. You should be getting a dental exam and cleaning every six months with dental x-rays annually. Teeth are essential to speaking and eating, to name a few. Some people neglect this, but if you're living your best life, you'll be smiling a lot. Guess what will be focused on while you are smiling? You're right; it's your teeth.

On the other hand, neglected dental issues can lead to more serious conditions. Once, I had a patient who failed to get treatment when she developed a tooth abscess. She ended up being admitted to the ICU with a tracheostomy after the abscess traveled to her throat and cut off her airway. I don't want to scare you, but it's important to help you see the importance of this aspect of physical wealth.

Symptom Management

Symptom management and monitoring is a collaborative effort between you and your care team. Your care team could include your primary care provider and other disciplines specializing in your symptoms or illnesses. I want to encourage you to get any symptoms you're experiencing evaluated. Don't ignore symptoms because most conditions can have better outcomes when they're detected early.

The first step in symptom management is recognizing when something is abnormal based on what you have been educated or trained on. There are digital tools to manage and monitor your symptoms. A popular and super cool tool right now is a continuous glucose monitor (CGM). This skin patch with a microneedle is a digital tool that prevents finger sticks and connects to a mobile app so a blood sugar measurement can happen at any time. You might require medications and supplements for symptom management and monitoring. Over-the-counter medications and supplements are usually the first options, but sometimes prescriptions are necessary.

Dietary Intake

Diet is a vital contributor to physical wealth. Diet is what you eat and can be anything. Your diet can be regular, high protein, low fat, low calorie, vegan, gluten free, or fasting. You can be on any type of diet you desire or need to maintain your energy level or optimize physical wealth. Each person has unique food needs and should adjust their diet to feel good and have enough energy.

I won't be addressing macronutrients and micronutrients in this book, but I encourage you to discuss this with your primary care provider so you can plan to meet those with your diet or supplements. According to myplate.gov[5], each day, your regular diet should include the following:

- 2 cups of fruit
- 2 1/2 cups of vegetables
- 6 ounces of grains
- 5 1/2 ounces of protein
- 3 cups of dairy foods

Another vital contributor to physical wealth is exercise or activity. Everyone needs to incorporate a certain level of activity to measure your heart rate and calories burned. Can you believe that some people are so active, in their career, that they don't need to add any exercise to their daily routine? The latest recommendation is a goal of 150 minutes of cardio exercise each week. The experts say this can be accumulative and doesn't need to happen at one time. For example, you can exercise in ten-minute increments during the week, and it'll all add up for your benefit. Also, physical exercise can be a stress reliever and be used as a coping mechanism. Having strong physical wealth is the foundation for the other three types of wealth.

Financial Wealth

Strong financial wealth lays the groundwork for social and time wealth. Financial wealth includes many indicators. The main indicators I focus on are income, credit, net worth, budgeting, debt-to-income ratio, savings, debt, and investing. I'm not a financial advisor or expert, but I want to share what I've discovered on my journey and what has worked for me. Hopefully, these nuggets will help you as much as they helped me. Remember that strength in all four types of wealth creates resilience to the S's.

Income

Your income is how much you earn. This includes earnings from an employer or entrepreneurship. What you make from an employer is usually capped, and you're basically trading time for money. As an entrepreneur, there's no cap, but you have to be engaged with your customers to make sure you're getting and keeping customers to purchase your service or product.

The most important aspect of income is what you do with it. I've made $3.50 per hour and had less stress than I had when I began to make $45 per hour. We'll go into budgeting later, but I wanted to explain that income level has little to do with your financial wealth. You'll see why later in this chapter.

A major part of your resilience is creating multiple streams of income (the average millionaire has seven streams of income[6]). Think about how nervous you'd be if you lost your only source of income. Now, think about how anxious you'd be if you lost a source of income, but you had six more streams of income to rely on.

Credit

Credit involves a report and a score. It can get complex, but I'm going to do my best to keep it simple. There are three credit bureaus for personal credit and one for business credit. The personal credit bureaus are Equifax, Transunion, and Experian, each containing different information and scores. The breakdown is complicated, but basically, they apply your open and closed accounts, your payments, and your delinquencies into a formula to generate a score. Each bureau calculates the score differently, so it can be a difficult system to understand. Credit is important because it allows you to buy things, get financial approvals (loans, credit cards, accounts), get a job, and even get insurance. On your success journey, you'll need to do all of these things, and your credit needs to open doors for you, not close them. It's okay if your credit isn't perfect, but you need to know what kind of credit you have. If there's room for improvement, you can make a plan to do so.

Everyone can get a copy of their credit from each credit bureau for free annually. The website to request your annual report is annualcreditreport.com. The website for your free business credit report is nav.com. Some people request reports from all credit bureaus at the same time. Others stagger the request. For example, they may request information from Equifax in January, Transunion in May, and Experian in October. The free report will only be the credit report and doesn't include a credit score. There are multiple ways to get a free credit score. You can sign up for an account on Credit Karma or Credit Sesame. These are websites and mobile apps that allow you to monitor your vantage score. Also, some credit cards allow you to get a free credit score. I have a Discover Card and can get my FICO score each month through them. Credit scores range from 300 to 850. Here is the breakdown:

300–641=poor
641–700=fair
701–750= good
751–850=excellent

If you have a less than desired credit score, this is what helped me get my score from the 500s to the 700s. First, I disputed all the inaccurate negative items. Next, I had all of the collection accounts removed after I paid them off. I opened a credit card and only used it for gas. Each month, I fully paid it off. I opened another credit card account to use for a low-cost subscription, less than $20. This card was paid in full each month as well. With this card, I did one thing different: I used my financial institution to pay it automatically with bill pay. So, I never had to worry about it. My credit score jumped like crazy. I don't want to encourage you to get a bunch of credit card debt. Keep in mind I paid these cards off monthly. If you can't pay off the credit cards each month, try your very best to keep the balance less than 30% of the limit. Anytime you let your balance go over 30%, it can negatively affect your score.

The provided guidelines for how they calculate your credit score is

Payment History—35%
Amount Owed—30%
Credit History—15%

New Credit—10%
Type of Credit—10%

You need to review your credit report so you can evaluate how to improve it. The first thing you want to do when you get your credit report is to check it for accuracy. If you find any inaccurate information, you should dispute it with the credit bureau. If you have negative items on your credit report, you want to make sure you look at each in detail and dispute any inaccurate information. The negative items will be on your report from seven to ten years based on what it is. Public record items, like judgments or bankruptcy, will be reported for ten years. If you see anything negative that's still being reported but has met the time requirement, dispute it. Sometimes, you have to remind the credit bureaus of items that should be off.

Check for collection accounts. A collection agency is a company lenders use to recover past-due funds. Once a creditor hires them (or, more accurately, sells your account to them), they create an account and report it to the credit bureau. One crucial thing most people don't know is collections are not required to be reported to the credit bureaus. They only report to the credit bureau to encourage you to pay the debt. You can remove these accounts, but it must be strategic. The best way to get a collection taken off your credit report is to get the agency to agree to remove the account if you pay the debt. I made the mistake of paying the debt first. There was no incentive for the collection agency to remove the account. Remember, their goal is getting the debt paid. I was successful in getting the collection removed after full payment because I was persistent. I sent a letter every month for three months requesting they remove the account. I was organized and set up a reminder on my calendar. After the third month, the collection agency complied with my request. I gave them a taste of their own medicine. The ultimate goal is to only have good items on your credit report. Get a copy of your credit report/score and get to work. This is a crucial step for your success plan.

Net Worth

Net worth is essential for getting approved for lending. Business lending almost always requires a net worth calculation. Net worth is assets minus liabilities—and the goal is for your net worth to be four times your income. Assets are what you own, and liabilities are what you owe. There's an example and a worksheet you can download and use to calculate your net worth on my website, Jamesharossrn.com. I encourage you to pause here and do this exercise.

Now that you've completed the exercise, is your net worth four times your income? If not, what can you do to increase your net worth?

Budgeting

Budgeting is an art. First, you have to make a budget. Then you have to find a way to operate your household within the budget. Before you start reviewing the recommended guidelines for your budget, let's see what you spend your money on. The suggestion is to keep a money journal for a week. This means writing down every dollar you spend: what you bought, where you spent the money, and how much you spent. After doing this, some people are shocked at how much money they spend on fast food and gas. I couldn't stay consistent when I tried to write the spending down at the time of purchase. One of the best things that helped me stick to my money journal for a week was keeping all my receipts and writing them down in a pocket-sized notebook at the end of the day. Add up your spending and put it to the side. Next, get your checking account statement and write those amounts down, too, but categorize the money coming out of your checking account. Now, combine what you have from spending (cash and credit) with your checking account spending. For some people, this is important because they have automatic payments set up for different accounts. Categorize your transactions into the groups below to make it easier to compare your spending with the recommended budget percentages. Compare your totals with the budget recommendations below. Here are the recommendations for how to create your budget. Take your income and divide it up into these percentages.

- 35%—Housing
- 10–20%—Food
- 15–20%—Transportation
- 5%—Insurance
- 5–15%—Debt
- 5–10%—Entertainment
- 3–5%—Clothing
- 5–10%—Family/Medical/Professional
- 5–10%—Personal

This breakdown is a reality check for some. Are you operating within the recommended budget percentages? Where do you need to make adjustments? Staying within budget takes discipline. I have practiced a three-question requirement to help keep myself focused when I purchase something. I ask myself if the purchase is a need, a want, or a love. A need is pretty self-explanatory. A want is something that you want, like a purse or new outfit. A love is something you're passionate about. I love to travel. First, I need to meet my needs. But after that, would you rather spend your money on wants or be strategic and spend your money on what you love? Sometimes, there can be overlap. I previously mentioned a purse was a want, but in some cases, it's a need. Our purses get worn out and tear up. In that case, a new purse would be a need. Start by asking yourself if your purchase is necessary and if it will keep you within your budget.

Debt

There are two types of debt: good debt and bad debt. The only difference is good debt generates income, and bad debt does not. How much debt do you have that's not generating income for you? One may have a goal of only having good debt, but most of us only have bad debt. That's okay. There's a strategy to eliminate bad debt.

This concept of good and bad debt can be confusing for some people, so let me break it down. If you're paying a mortgage on your primary home and not making money on it, that's a bad debt. I didn't say it wasn't an investment. If you're buying your home, you have invested in it and probably have equity. Home equity is when your home is worth more than what you owe. Equity is a plus for your net worth we discussed and calculated earlier.

If you have purchased a rental property and are financing it, this is good debt as long as you have renters. The rental property is generating income through the rent payments. Some people have figured out how to house hack. If you don't know what house hacking is, let me shed some light on it. A person can purchase a multifamily home—a duplex or triplex—and rent out the vacant unit. The rent payment for the vacant unit can be enough to cover the mortgage and then some. This means the owner generates income from their primary home. If you have more questions about this, look up house hacking, and you can find out more information about how you can do it.

Let's switch it up and discuss how you can eliminate bad debt. There are lots of approaches to debt. I'll share what has worked for me. I have used the debt-snowball method, debt-avalanche method, restructuring-debt method, and interest-reduction method. The debt-snowball method involves you listing out your debt along with the minimum payments. Start eliminating one debt at a time. You'll pay off the lowest debt first. All the other debt will only get the minimum payment. After you pay off the lowest account balance, the money you put towards it will then go towards payments on the next highest account balance. You'll repeat this process until you pay off all your accounts. There will be momentum as you start to see accounts paid in full while eliminating your bad debt.

The debt-avalanche method is very similar to the debt snowball method. The only difference is the debt is paid from the highest interest rate to the lowest interest rate. Instead of paying the account with the smallest balance first, you pay the one with the highest interest rate first.

Debt restructuring means exactly what it says: restructuring all your debt. When I restructured mine, I consolidated my student loans to get a better interest rate and make one payment instead of three. I restructured my high-interest credit cards to a personal loan. That gave me one payment for three years instead of one per credit card. I still had the debt, but I was paying 9% with my consolidation loan instead of 20%.

The last debt eliminating method is the rate-reduction method. I called all of my high-interest credit cards and requested a reduced rate. I was asking for this based on my payment history being perfect and the age of my account. Some phone calls were easier than others. For example, some of my credit card companies agreed to my request. Others compromised and only gave me a rate reduction for six months to a year. Some companies told me no, but I didn't just take no for an answer. (Come on! You know how determined I am.) If the first rep said no, I asked for a supervisor. If the supervisor said no, I asked for the manager. No to me only means not right now—I'll keep trying. If all three levels denied my request, I put a reminder on my calendar to call back and repeat my request in six months. Don't be afraid to ask for what you want. All they can say is no. Just remember not to take it personally. If you never ask, you'll never know what's possible.

Eliminating debt isn't easy—it's a balancing act. While eliminating bad debt, you don't want to be so focused on debt that you don't start investing. The reality is there are lots of people who are debt-free and are far from meeting their needs, which isn't helping them become their best version. We'll be touching on investment next because that's the other component to balance with bad debt.

Debt-to-Income Ratio

Lending decisions require an evaluation of your debt-to-income ratio. This ratio is your monthly payments divided by your monthly income (payments/income). The goal for this number is 36–43%. You'll need to list out all of your payments and add them up. Then add up all of your income for one month. Divide your payments by your income, and there you have it. Most lenders won't approve you unless it is under 40%. Is it within the suggested range? If not, what can you do to get in the range? Either you need to spend less or make more.

I recommend you do what I do each year. I get new quotes on my insurance policies to see if I can capture a savings. Also, I call my cell phone company and cable/internet company to see if I can take advantage of any bundles or specials. After that, I take a good look at everything I'm paying to see what's necessary and what I can eliminate. One year, I decided to end my gym membership and go to the local park to exercise and take advantage of community events that would increase my activity. We have an area downtown that hosts exercise in the park. It's really cool and free, and you get to meet new people.

Savings

Savings breaks down into two categories for me: emergency savings and savings, savings. The best approach to savings is to pay yourself first. Your money should be going to savings before any of your expenses. Consistency is the key. The system that works for me involves two savings accounts. The savings account at my primary bank is my emergency savings. I started with a goal of $1,000, dedicating $100 from each paycheck into the account. Anything over that goal is what I called a cushion. The good thing about the emergency savings account being at my primary bank is easy access. I could get to the money quickly if I had an emergency. Now, let's talk about what an emergency is. In my life, something like a flat tire while I'm traveling and am forced to buy a new tire on a short notice constitutes an emergency. It's impossible for me to shop around. So, I have to get towed and buy a tire immediately so my road trip can continue.

The savings, savings is different. It's an online account and not for emergency use—it's for my savings goals, to fund my passions, or for my loves. There isn't a debit card tied to this account. I have to make deposits and withdrawals electronically, and it takes a week to get the money from it. This money is your safety net. It'll give you comfort to know that if something catastrophic happens in your life, you'll be able to lean on your savings, savings. In addition to your responsibility are your passions and loves, like my girls' trip or my next innovative idea.

The goal for this account should be enough to cover six months of expenses. I don't touch this money until I reach my goal, and I've shopped around to get the best rates or the best manufacturer. This goal does not happen overnight, or even within one year in most cases. It's a long-term goal. The best thing about this savings account is the interest rates for online accounts are usually more than brick-and-mortar savings accounts. The interest rate at my primary financial institution is 0.20%—the savings interest rate for my online bank is currently 0.50%. When I opened my online savings account, it was 2.1%. I suggest that you monitor rates and make the best decision for you. Interest rates change frequently. Again, I am not a financial advisor. I am sharing what has helped me in hopes that it will help you.

You know I have to add some really cool innovative options into the mix. If saving is your weakness and you struggle with it, there are apps that can help you save. It can be helpful to have the money removed from your account without you manually doing it. The app links to your accounts, but after that, it'll move money out of your checking account and save it for you. There's one particular app I won't mention by name, but it uses a formula that involves the change leftover when you buy something. For example, when you use your debit card to purchase something that cost $1.77, the app will take the amount that would round up to the nearest dollar and save it for you. Believe it or not, it actually works. The dollar amount is so small that you don't miss it. The app sends you updates on your savings total. You can save without trying to save, and you can always return the money to your checking account the same day if necessary. What is your goal for both types of savings?

Investment

This section is not about advising on investments. It'll be a guide to doing more research on this topic so you can make investment decisions. I want to share my investment strategies with you. I have invested in myself. My education is a priority for my investments. I've invested in formal education and non-traditional information to help me get to the next level. I have invested in mentors and coaching. The best way to understand investing in you to become your best version is that Rory Vaden quote I love: "Success is never owned. It is only rented, and the rent is due every day." Just think about that for a moment.

I have invested in businesses. Yes, I've owned multiple businesses. Some succeeded, and some haven't been so successful. I learned what I was supposed to from each business. If you're not an entrepreneur, I suggest you explore how you can become one. Business ideas are simple if you stick to the basics. What can you do to solve a problem, make something easier, or improve an experience? There's always room for improvement, even if you think the market is saturated. Also, think of a product or service that you love doing or talking about. If you're doing what you love or have a passion for, the money will follow. What are some things you're passionate about? Can you offer this service or product and make a profit? It has to make sense for you to be in business. Otherwise, it's just a hobby, and you're essentially volunteering.

With the popularity of property flipping and increased residential developments, property investment is really hot right now. I entered into property flipping with some hesitation, but I loved it! On my first flip, I was made aware by a family member of a homeowner in my neighborhood wanting to sell. The house was a total rehab that I purchased for $5,000. When I made the offer, I didn't have $5,000. I entered a contract with the owner with half down and the balance paid in thirty days. I renovated and updated the home at a cost of $70,000 through a combination of savings and credit. The house sold for $139,000. Then I used the proceeds from that sale to purchase the next flip project. If you can find a sweet spot in your city, you can flip homes successfully. The sweet spot neighborhood you want to find has a combination of owned and rented homes. The value of the homes in these neighborhoods will jump as the old homes are being updated and sold. The neighborhood I was investing in had an average price of $125 per square foot, and the average length of time on the market was less than thirty days.

Rental property is also a form of property investment you can finance. It's commercial lending if you are financing a rental property. If you don't have the means to finance a rental property, there's still another way to purchase property at a discount. Properties are sold at property tax auctions. A property tax auction is an auction of property delinquent in property taxes for at least three years. Where I live, the county accessor manages this auction, and it only happens once a year. Their website lists the auction properties, and anyone can bid. These houses usually need a great deal of work. You might get blessed with a home that's livable or has someone living in it. The bidding starts at what the delinquent tax balance is. Typical bid awards range from $2,500-$20,000. I encourage you to see how your county handles delinquent property taxes because you may be able to invest in property with a small amount of money.

Stocks and Bonds

Don't forget about stocks and bonds. If you have a retirement savings account, the investment firm probably invests it in a combination of stocks and bonds. There's a great deal of information on stocks and bonds available on the internet. Some stocks have voting rights, others have dividends, and the list goes on. There are even mobile applications teaching how to invest with little money and changing the investment landscape.

I added this section to encourage you to do more research and use the available technology to invest.

Cryptocurrency and Foreign Exchange

I couldn't end this section without mentioning cryptocurrency and foreign exchange. I remember when Bitcoin came out. It was so unfamiliar to me that I couldn't grasp the concept. I hate that I didn't take the time to understand it so I could invest in it. Now, all the first investors are sitting with deep pockets. I have no experience with cryptocurrency investment or foreign exchange. I know a good friend who's having huge success with foreign exchange. Because I know people who've succeeded with both of these types of investments, I added them to the section as an encouragement to include them in your investment research before you make an investment decision. Keep in mind that all investment comes with a risk. If someone tells you that an investment is guaranteed to provide you with a certain payoff, I would proceed cautiously.

Investing will be another stream of income if you do it strategically and properly. I added this investment section because it's critical for you to invest in something, even if it's only yourself.

Time Wealth

Freedom, knowledge, and abundance are three factors of time wealth. What does time mean to you? Imagine being in control of your time. Please don't confuse time wealth with time management. Time management is a totally different concept that we covered in a previous chapter. Go back and review it if you want more clarity on time management. Many of us are trading time for other things. People trade time for money, like on a job. When you accomplish time wealth, you can go and come as you please. You own your time to do what you will. When you have time wealth, no time is wasted because you're making the most of it. Imagine a day when each moment of your time is intentional. Now, think about what you'd eliminate. What would you be doing with your time? What would you stop doing?

Accomplishing time wealth is more than just relaxing. You use your time to do what is in alignment with your God-given purpose. You're making an impact in the world, leaving your legacy, and inspiring others. When you meet your needs and you have time wealth, you're in a position to fill the gap for someone else.

What would you be doing if you accomplished time wealth? I usually ask this question when I am interviewing someone. It gives me insight into what makes their heart sing. For me, I would be helping single mothers accomplish goals and get to the next level in life. It's my passion. I never get tired of seeing women figure it out and doing whatever it is they're supposed to be doing. So, I have that question for you. What would you do with your time? What can you do all day and never get tired of doing it or talking about it?

Knowledge allows you to have more time at your disposal. Think about the last time you bought a piece of furniture that required assembly. Before you could start putting it together, you had to read the instructions a few times. I have to read the package insert a few times to make sure I have all the required tools and understand the instructions well enough to do it alone—it's a time-consuming process. But if you know how to put the furniture together, you start separating the parts and lining everything up, and you're done in no time. That's an example of how knowledge can lead to time wealth.

Another example of how you can save time with knowledge is by getting a mentor or coach. I have several coaches. I'm a firm believer in obtaining information and skill from someone who has accomplished what I want to achieve. The key is getting the right coach/mentor. You want a mentor you can vibe with, just like with anything else in life. You don't want to hire a doctor with a view on life that does not mesh well with yours. The only way you'll be able to find out if they're a fit is by asking questions. In

2020, I had three coaches at one time. All of them were women of color who were killing the game. They were all doing things I wanted to do. Now, I could have taken my time and learned how to do what I wanted to accomplish on my own. But I learned a long time ago you shorten the time to your goals by learning from a coach or mentor. I have that same advice for you. You don't have to do this alone; if you have the right coach/mentor, they will help you get the results you want faster.

An abundance of resources will create time wealth. Imagine being on vacation and not worrying about when you're returning. Have you ever been faced with changing your travel plans just because you want to? When it's time to catch your return flight, you call to reschedule, and you're not worried about how much it will cost. You're not concerned about how long you'll need to wait for the next flight. You are not worried about getting more clothing. Without abundance, your options would be very limited, if you have any options at all.

Another example is when you require healthcare. With abundance, you can choose your provider, your hospital, the scheduling of your procedure, and the amount of time off you take. Now, try to imagine picking the top-of-the-line surgeon—the best of the best. You'd be able to vet hospitals, tour the facility before your procedure, have the procedure when it worked best for you, and recover without being concerned about how you would continue to meet your needs. With abundant resources, you could get twenty-four-hour care in your home from nurses for wound care and physical therapist for mobility and strengthening. I want to see what you will do with abundance in your life without limits.

My grandmother was a custodian at a local college and a provider for two clients. She didn't make much money at all. She graduated from high school but didn't have any college education. She managed to juggle all three jobs, and on occasion, she'd go to all three jobs on the same day. However, she always had enough. I'm not sure how she could pay her bills and always be there for her kids, grandkids, nieces, and nephews. Remember, I spent a great deal of time with her. If anyone in the family needed a place to stay or food, she filled the gap. I can recall family members sleeping in the den for extended times. She made everyone feel at home. I really don't understand how she could work multiple jobs and have dinner on the table for us after school. It didn't matter how many people were visiting, we never ran out of food. She could make a pot of spaghetti and cornbread stretch for what seemed like forever. She created abundance with her resources and taught us by doing the impossible.

Sometimes, abundance is being able to appreciate what you have and being fulfilled with your resources. You make it enough. There's no endless bank account with a bunch of zeros, but all the bills are paid, and stomachs are full. This was it: enjoying life and living with freedom, knowledge, and abundance.

Social Wealth

Social wealth is the total value of status, influence, and relationships. Status is related to the social status of someone, which can come from a career, income, talent, car, parenthood, and many more things. Influence is related to how much impact a person has on others. Others can persuade people. Relationships are connections to other people. This can be family, friends, business partners, colleagues, or communities.

Social wealth is usually the last type of wealth to accomplish. That's because it usually depends on the strength of physical, financial, and time wealth. For example, have you ever been involved with a nonprofit fundraiser? It can be a show of social wealth. The fundraiser, in many cases, has a chairperson who's a person with status, influence, and relationships. I've been in a fundraiser meeting where the chairperson can make a phone call, request support, and get a $10,000 donation. This example is a simple depiction of social wealth. In that same organization, another person with social wealth was able to post on social media and get all of the volunteers for an event. I gave both of those examples because it is not all about money. It can be time or skills.

To gain strength in status, stay true to yourself. Make decisions that won't compromise who you are. Take pride in who you are, and don't feel like you have to buy anything (like food or alcohol) to please others or make them feel comfortable around you. Once, I was interviewing at a restaurant. A panel of employees was interviewing me. They all ordered seafood and alcohol, while I ordered chicken and water. I felt the energy at the table took a nosedive after that. At that moment, I felt different and like my social status dropped a few levels because of what I ordered. My order was a reflection of what I wanted to eat, and I stayed true to myself. After the dishes arrived, one of the ladies offered me mussels and oysters. For a moment, I thought about taking a risk and trying mussels, but I decided that it would be too uncomfortable, and I was more concerned about my confidence with the interview questions. By staying true to myself, I gained strength in status. Even though they didn't select me for the position, all of them admired my experience and skill set.

Status comes with involvement. Therefore, you can't gain status if you're not social. Character and passion also play a part in status. For example, you can gain status by leading a movement and being willing to fall on the sword for your beliefs. Many leaders gained status by standing up for change. Rosa Parks said no and triggered a national movement, a boycott. This simple act gained status for her and resulted in moving the needle on equality.

Some people feel the accomplishments of parents or children define status. In many cases, they think those accomplishments grant them privilege or special treatment. Others feel cars give them status. I used to drive a sexy, black, convertible Jaguar. I always felt the stares of other people trying to figure out what kind of car I was driving. It was a totally different response from when I was driving my Nissan Quest van. I wasn't turning any heads in my football mom van. There was a difference in how people treated and viewed me because of the status that came with driving a sporty vehicle versus a van.

You can influence a person by simply sharing your goals with them. I shared my goal of writing a book to share my testimony with my sister, and shortly afterward, she began working on her goal of writing a poetry book. I often influence her because I'm her older sister. Simply being sisters has influence. Most of the time, it's a positive influence but can be negative on some days.

I also want to clarify that being strong in one wealth category and weak in another isn't helpful for resilience. For example, a person with deep pockets or strong financial wealth can't be a person who makes people cringe when they enter the room. Keep all four types of wealth in mind on your journey and navigate success with strength in each.

CHAPTER 9

Motivation

Motivation is similar to the muscular system, which is responsible for moving your body. Muscles contract and expand and result in movement. For example, the shoulder muscles move your hands. Motivation moves you in the direction of your goals. What causes motivation? Sometimes, it comes from internal, and other times, it comes from external sources.

Internal motivation comes when your why is bigger than you. Remember why it's important for you to achieve your goals and become your visions.

Real-life has ups and downs, as we all know—it's unavoidable. The key is how long you're down. The amount of time you're in a downturn gets shorter as you develop more motivation. When a downturn is slowing your progress, you have to confront it. After facing it, identify the lesson, then get back on your feet. There's a song by a 90s R&B group, Jodeci, called "Get On Up." Google it if you haven't heard it. It's a perfect song to blast in the car when you know you've come too far to give up.

Success Mindset

When you decide losing isn't an option, it really isn't. When your mindset is on winning in every endeavor, it makes it easy to see the positive in each experience. There's positivity in each thing that we encounter. As a new nurse, I was forced to care for twelve patients at times. I was constantly working late. This created a negative experience for me. My twelve-hour shifts would turn into fourteen-hour shifts. The first and only time I cried at work was on a night I couldn't leave when my shift was over. After giving a report to the relieving nurse, I had to chart. My babysitter was calling me to get my kids. I knew I had at least two hours of charting to complete before I could leave. My babysitter was obviously frustrated with me when I told her I would be late again. I struggled with documenting the details of every event because I was mentally exhausted and torn down. This was definitely one of few shifts that prevented me from cracking a chart open because the urgency to care for patients overrode every attempt to chart. My bladder was about to burst from not being able to step foot in a restroom all shift. It was too much. When I hung up the phone with my babysitter, I sat there, trying to hold it together so I could leave, but the tears started falling. There was no sound, just tears. I discovered a new level of strength during that shift. I wasn't going to lose all my marbles that night, so I looked at the positive. My leadership and nursing skills were getting stronger. This growth didn't come without trauma—goal trauma.

I chose to win. I had to remember my why to get through most of those overloaded, long shifts. The nurse-to-patient ratio of 12:1 is unsafe. It forced me into survival mode so my patients could get well. It was risky. I mean the type of risk that caused me to be on the front line of life and death every shift. I was traumatized by the pressure of keeping my patients alive during my shift with minimal support. I was disappointed with my career, but I didn't let it stop me. I made a choice to leave that facility when my role no longer served me.

I experienced a form of goal trauma. Goal trauma is what you experience when things do not happen the way you want while pursuing goals. I had a goal of becoming a nurse. I accomplished this with kids. But I wasn't happy with my nursing job and was at risk of changing careers. One of the things I love about nursing is that you can still be a nurse and totally change specialties. I was able to fall back in love with nursing by changing organizations and specialties.

Sometimes, goal trauma can happen before you complete your goal. Many things made it hard to complete my goals, but I never let those things stop me from going to class or completing my clinicals. All the bumps and bruises you get from the delays and detours of your journey are meant to be. Everything happens for a reason.

During my last semester of prerequisites, I had to add another science class with a lab to my schedule. I was taking General Physiology, Anatomy and Physiology, and Microbiology. That was insane. Like, I had too many labs, and each lab required a lab report. The goal trauma from being overloaded during school prepared me for the pressure of nursing school but also prevented me from retaining all the material—it was just too much information to digest. As a college student, I looked forward to reselling my textbooks to the bookstore at the end of the semester. It provided extra cash I needed desperately. One book was the equivalent to gas or groceries. I kept all those books when the semester was over because I had a feeling I would need to reference them later—and I did. I spent time reviewing some topics later. So, when those mishaps happen, take comfort in accepting that it's happening to prepare you for something that you'll face in the future.

Why not start making your goals real today? Just start. If you haven't started, make today the first day. Do it scared, alone, or whatever state you're in right now. Some people may disagree with this, but I think you have to fake it until you make it. You won't have all of the answers when you start, but you'll find them. The answer could very well be how much you'll charge for your services or what you'll offer. You'll get to the details when the time comes.

Now, let's back up for a moment. I'm not saying be dishonest. Be truthful so you can earn trust. What I *am* saying is the first time you do something, you might have to present yourself in a manner that illustrates you have experience. For example, my first time giving a demo of my mobile app, I had to present myself as a seasoned app professional so the potential buyer would have confidence in me and the value of my mobile app. You'll find yourself in situations requiring you to be confident on the outside even though you are screaming on the inside. I repeat: <u>fake it until you make it</u>.

Progress Over Perfection

Progress over perfection will become your approach to everything. It'll be necessary to keep you from getting stuck. Perfection doesn't exist with success. No one is perfect but the Lord. There's always room for improvement, but if you're waiting for the ideal time to do something, it'll never come. At any given moment, you'll be able to identify something that could be better. This doesn't mean you won't look at situations and say to yourself, "The timing was perfect." It seems like divine intervention happens sometimes. For example, my best friend's daughter decided to explore art and decided she liked it. This coincided almost exactly when I was finishing my book and needed an illustrator. It felt like perfect timing.

Progress can feel like baby steps sometimes. When I was stepping out on faith to create an app, I wasn't super happy with my first version. But I was pleased I was making progress. I started. I was afraid, but I kept going. I struggled with defining what I wanted the app to do and what problem it would solve. Each time I addressed the app, I made progress. When I sent my first email campaign to potential customers, my heart was beating so fast I had to stand up when I hit the send button. I was terrified that once I sent the email into the matrix of electronic communication, I would have to face the reality of rejection, being ignored, or answered. Out of 200 emails, I scheduled five phone calls to gauge what my potential customers' needs were and demo the app. Each time I did a call and demo, I felt like I got better. It became easier to articulate my words and understand their needs. Those were my baby steps.

I used a software program to track each email campaign. It could track when someone opened an email, when they clicked a link within the email, or when someone replied to it. Even though I was only taking baby steps, I celebrated each time someone opened an email. I gave myself a high five each time I received a reply. Some of the replies were to tell me they weren't interested and stop sending emails. Still, it was progress to have another person read about what I was doing, and if they ever get to a point where they need an app like mine to serve their needs, they might contact me. Understanding the magnitude of awareness was progress. I never thought about how much effort it would take to acquire a customer in the competitive world of technology.

Daily effort is required to recognize progress and celebrate it daily. Progress over perfection is crucial in keeping the momentum of your goals and success. I have an oath all my clients take. It's the "progress over perfection" oath. It would be ideal for you to take this oath as well. Here's how it should go. You stand in the mirror with your left hand raised as if swearing under oath. Put your right hand on your heart. Now, repeat after me: "I, *your name*, will not get caught up in trying to make things perfect. I will demand progress every day and celebrate all progress no matter how small." Remember that you took an oath, and you have to act accordingly.

Un-Network

Un-networking is the opposite of networking. The people who are around you on your success journey are important. Those people can hold you back or help you accelerate. Many people think you're the product of your five closest friends. Take a moment to reflect on who are your five closest friends. Then do an inventory of what makes them who they are. What are their strengths, weaknesses, values, priorities, and goals? Don't do this with any comparison to you—evaluate each person as an individual. As you go down the list of strengths and weaknesses of your friends, do you notice any trends? What do you all have in common? What are your friends doing to prepare them for the opportunity to leap to the next level? How can you all help each other? What weaknesses do you have that are strengths for someone else? What strengths do you have that are weaknesses for someone else? If you find that your inventory of your friends is not a list of strengths and weaknesses that can complement each other, then your friend list needs to change. Sometimes, a difference of purpose and outlook on life can be enough to initiate un-networking. I'm not saying you only need to be around people exactly like you or you need to eliminate the weakest link. Just be mindful of who you're sharing your time and energy with.

Sharing your goals or vision with others can be scary. The person who you're sharing with could be negative and discouraging. Think about how it would affect a preschool student if their teacher asked, "What do you want to be when you grow up?" The preschooler would be super excited to share and would proudly say, "I want to be a donut taster." There's a variety of possible responses from the teacher. The wrong response can destroy the child's imagination and vision for the future. The right one can give the preschooler the fuel to hope and keep the dream alive. The teacher's reply could be "that's great! You can be anything that you put your mind to" or "think of a different job." Either way, the response will have an impact on the student's imagination.

Believe it or not, some people around you can't imagine or process your goals and visions. Some people have limiting thoughts of themselves, which makes it impossible for them to process you actually accomplishing your goals. When I graduated, most people were happy for me and congratulated me for the huge accomplishment of graduating from nursing school with kids.

But I had a few friends who weren't exactly happy. They wanted to know how I was able to do it. Not only did I succeed with kids, but I also finished with them knowing where I came from.

Recall life events you were excited about and make a note of who wasn't happy with you when you shared your life event. You might have to really lean on your memory for this. Cutting ties with the people around you who don't seem to align with what you need to serve you is a symbol of growth. Removing those people from your life isn't an easy task, but growth is often uncomfortable. One way to cut ties with someone or un-network is to establish boundaries. Telling people you're not available won't be enough, but letting them know you won't be gossiping with them anymore because it no longer serves you will be enough. Be specific so there's no room for confusion. With that statement, you're not telling them to stop gossiping, but you're making it very clear that you won't be doing it with them anymore. They have a choice: they can call you with better things to discuss or not call you. My point is, there's no room for interpretation. You've provided a boundary and an explanation for it.

Another way to un-network is through invitation. If you invite someone to a fundraiser to volunteer, a meeting, or an event and that person has no interest, they'll find a way to create distance from you. The pressure of doing something in alignment with you but not within their realm of being will cause them to generate distance from you. The invitations will be a mechanism to end the connection. It really works.

Having high expectations for yourself spills into your network. Your expectations of others elevates them to a new level. This will result in people stepping their game up or falling off. This falling off is another way of un-networking.

Rejection

Rejection is necessary to become your best version, but most of us don't know how to deal with it. You'll hear "no," "hell no," and even "hell to the no, Bobby." These are all variations of being told no. In being your best version, being told no only means not right now—just like when I was trying to get my credit card rates lowered. The only difference between how a TTGer and TTSer reacts to being told no is simple. A TTSer will let a "no" stop them from trying to accomplish a goal or get to the next level of success. A TTGer will interpret a "no" as not right now and will use it to explore how to get things done another way. Once I understood that concept, I was unstoppable. I was creative. Still, finding a way out of "no way" was a challenge.

One of my vital needs is volunteering. I spend a lot of time asking for donations for fundraiser events. For example, if I'm trying to get a donation for an event, there is a high probability that half of the people will decline to donate. In some extreme cases, every person may refuse to contribute.

The first step to accepting rejection is to get more practice asking for things and take the risk of getting rejected. This can be as simple as asking for things throughout the day. When you go to a store, ask for a discount or ask for a price comparison. All they can say is no. If the store clerk says no, you pay full price or choose not to buy the item. In many cases, you'll eventually get a yes. This exercise will help you get thicker skin and understand being rejected or told "no" isn't the end of the world. It can actually be a source of motivation. This type of motivation stems from wanting to do what you have been told you can't do or what seems impossible. The urge to prove the concept overcomes fear.

It is crucial not to let rejection discourage you. Stay faithful to your goals and ultimate success. Keep preparing yourself and doing what it takes so when given the opportunity, you can secure the traction your goal needs at that moment. One example is when you're trying to get accepted into nursing school. The first school you apply for may deny your application for admission. While looking for another school to apply to, you may start looking for a job in the healthcare field. This job could expose you to learning opportunities that will help prepare you for nursing school. For example, a job in a pharmacy could better prepare you for pharmacology classes or educating patients on medication side effects. Think about what you could be doing to put yourself in a better position after being rejected.

In addition to getting thicker skin, you could learn to embrace and reflect on why the rejection happened. Was it your delivery? Lack of confidence? Did you lack experience? If you can pinpoint the reason, you can start focusing on ways to overcome it. It may be as simple as getting a coach or mentor to help with areas that need strengthening. If it's a simple lack of experience, you may be able to offer your expertise for free to a small group to gain more experience. It could be a win-win situation.

CHAPTER 10

Inspire: Your Highest Level of Success

What is success? Some people think success is money and material things. Success has different meanings for everyone. It really boils down to how you can inspire others. If you're making lots of money and spending it on your desires, but you're despised, how does that translate to being able to inspire others? As we take small steps toward our goals, people zone in on who we are and less on what we do. When I started my nursing career, I was a graduate nurse. No one knew what kind of nurse I would be, but I passed my boards and now have a license to practice as a nurse. As a seasoned nurse, I'm known for being a patient advocate and passionate. I was filled with joy and gratitude when I hit the floor, and it showed. My patients were happy to see a nurse smiling, eager to care for them, and anticipating their needs. At some point, I transformed from a nurse to a passionate, strong nurse. I became known for who I am.

There will be a pivotal moment in your life that will take your identity from what you do to who you are. That's the moment you'll inspire the people around you. Outside of nursing, my identity includes many things, but most people know me as a fearless and strong woman of color who has broken boundaries.

What do people know about you right now? What do you want people to know about you? It takes courage to share your survivals and humble brags. When you open it up, there could be some negativity that comes your way. The feedback could include judgment. I used to get embarrassed when I revealed my oldest daughter's age. I was ashamed of having a child at fifteen years of age. I didn't want people to judge me. When I realized being a teen mom helped me prepare for what was ahead of me, I started to embrace and own it. It is what it is. It is my story, and I know for sure that facing the dilemmas and experiencing the responsibility of another life at a young age shaped who I am today.

The moments that challenged your beliefs and stretched you beyond your comfort zone are the moments that will inspire others. Most of those moments involved some element that was larger than you. Things bigger than us drive us. As a teen mom, that element was my daughter. She was my motivation. As a nursepreneur, that element was being able to break cycles of poverty and survival mode. I want my great-grandchildren to have confidence, resilience, and motivation. That stems from my actions and the legacy that I leave. Obtain the attention of other people by doing something you're not supposed to do. They'll listen, connect with you, and in many cases, want to work with you.

When you were around the age of five, think about the people who inspired you. Who helped or protected you? Who came to your rescue when you needed saving? Did someone make you feel like you could do anything? It could've been someone who helped you wash your hands so you wouldn't get dirt into your eyes. Or maybe it was a person who decided to give you their old books instead of selling them back to the bookstore. That person was your first success hero.

We all have success heroes. My grandmother was one of mine. She taught me how to balance her checkbook and how to write checks for all of her bills. She helped me open a checking account once I was sixteen years old. I still have that checking account. She would let me buy designer clothes on her charge cards. She would often tell me, "Buy what you want now because you'll have to sacrifice later." I didn't know what she meant at the time, but as an adult, I fully understand. She loved to cook, and she had an open door for anyone who needed help. There were times when a family member would ask her for money, and she would get it even if she had to take out a loan. As she succumbed to Alzheimer's, she still tried to help everyone she could.

Grandma was truly a jewel for our family. She used to take me to work with her, and I would help her clean sometimes. She was laying a foundation of hard work and responsibility. I never wanted to go home. I would cry when it was time to go home. My sister and I loved getting to stay with my grandmother while my mother worked long hours at the post office. Apparently, it was a good job. When she was laid off, our lives changed. I could tell that our struggle was about to be real. We moved out of our house and into one of the family houses. The family had an undercurrent of tension and rivalry as my grandmother's health started to decline. My grandmother would eventually need the care of her family when Alzheimer's took over her life. She could no longer manage her needs. The conflict interfered with the family working together to care for her, and when she died, some of her children weren't even talking to each other. She would have been extremely disappointed about that. It still doesn't seem real. The queen of my existence is gone, and I can't call her and tell her what is going on. She always knew what to say to make me feel like I could conquer the world, and everything would be okay. I just want to take a moment to reflect on how I wasn't supposed to finish high school, but not only did I finish, but I finished on time. Sometimes, I have to remember how impossible it felt at the time to get up for school and stay up to finish homework. Just this recall helps me remember how strong I am and that I can do anything that I am determined to do. So can you.

I was my mother's oldest child and had to be responsible for my younger sisters. I used to babysit them and my cousins. I knew how to keep order and do what needed to be done. This organic skill translates to leadership skills in the current world. Did you have a natural skill that outshined your other skills as a kid that you still use today?

I didn't let my motherhood stop me from finishing high school on time. I decided to go to college the fall after high school. At first, I thought I wanted to be a chemical engineer because I loved chemistry. Then I decided to be a pharmacist, but it would've required me to move to Oklahoma City. So, I changed to nursing because it just felt natural to stay in Tulsa with my daughter, and I wanted to make people feel like the neonatal nurses made me feel.

I had an aggressive schedule, and it wasn't easy to go to college full time, work part time, and have time to hang out with my friends. I was doing something every day of the week. Mondays and Tuesdays, I had class. Clinicals happened on Thursdays and Fridays. On the weekends, I worked twelve-hour shifts at a tow truck company. My grind was official—there was no downtime. It was all gas and no brakes until I graduated. When I was tired, I reminded myself I had to stay on course for four years. Four years of sacrifice, tears at times, sleep deprivation most of the time, and lots of determination.

As I mentioned before, I used all of the available community resources while in school. I received TANF at a point. I was on Section 8 with rental and utility assistance. Additionally, I had WIC and food stamps, daycare assistance, and Title 19 for insurance. Because resources were scarce, I had to call every month to make payment arrangements on my utilities and sometimes even had to stand in line at agencies to get my bills paid. I had to go to Emergency Infant Services for diapers and formula. I was broker than broke. It was normal to rob Peter to pay Paul.

I had faith, and that was because of my grandmother. She made sure that I knew nothing was impossible with God. I knew that God would make a way for me.

I couldn't think of anything else but finishing school. I had to do it for my children. Yes, I went on to have three more children with my childhood sweetheart. We got married after the fourth child. It wore me out at times, but I couldn't give up. I had to stay up all night some nights just to finish my work. Thankfully, it was a family affair that allowed me quality time with them. My children and boyfriend were often my fake patients to practice assessment skills on, and they would help me make posters for presentations. Since I hated that knot in the pit of my stomach when the teacher asked for assignments and I didn't have my work completed, it was worth it to stay up after the kids went to sleep just so I could turn in my work.

I was the youngest person in my nursing class, but it didn't stop me. I knew I would finish. One instructor told me I should consider taking off the last semester of nursing school because I was pregnant with my daughter Jada. I wasn't going to let pregnancy stop me. I delivered Jada on a Saturday and was back in clinicals Thursday. My sister, LaTeesch, agreed to come to my house and keep my newborn while I was in class. That really saved me. It takes a village.

Throughout high school and college, my family helped me with my children. I graduated from nursing school with an eight-year-old, four-year-old, and a three-month-old. I was finally going to be able to pay my rent, buy groceries, pay the *whole* utility bill each month. I also had money to buy all of the school supplies before school started, fill my tank up, keep my checking account from going negative, and pay people back for the money I had borrowed.

The ups and downs in life don't stop. Sometimes, you take a few steps forward, and then you take a few steps back. This back and forth in life doesn't change. The only thing that changes is the caliber of steps. In the beginning stages of my life, those steps could represent my daughter getting sick and causing me to miss class and makeup work. In the current state, a step back could be that my property didn't appraise at or above the asking price. We just find a way to do what needs to be done.

If you ever hit a delay, just figure out how you can resolve the issue. This was just like how I worked out an agreement for my sister to care for my daughter so that I could get back to clinicals. Otherwise, I would've had to wait six weeks for her to get enrolled in a daycare.

First, you have to be your own success hero, meaning you have to be proud of where you are. Don't forget where you came from but pat yourself on the back and say, "I did that!" No one is going to be inspired by you until you're inspired by you. Then you get to be someone else's success hero. You may not know who you have inspired, but I'm pretty sure that you have inspired someone. Pay attention to who is asking you how to do things or for advice. It can easily be your child or a child who has been around you. A family member or friend has most likely experienced a feeling while in your presence. That feeling could have been empowerment or encouragement and could lead to them taking action or the first step toward a goal. I can usually tell who is paying attention to my actions. Who is watching and making sure they're there to assist with tasks?

I often get questions about how I was able to buy my first home. This question would only come from someone who hasn't accomplished this milestone in life. I get this question because I have shared I own my home with someone at some point. Not everyone accomplishes homeownership. Some people don't have the desire or priority to purchase a home. Everyone has their reasons for what they choose to do, but my point is your testimony will trigger people to ask questions when you inspire them.

People should be inspired by how you can strategize and build a foundation while breaking bad habits and ending bad cycles. Part of being able to inspire others is sharing your story. Your story is your testimony. This can be in the form of sharing how you overcame obstacles, challenges, and accomplishments. No huge platform is required. It can be word of mouth. A one-on-one conversation will do any day.

There are many platforms for you to share your testimony. For example, social media. There's Facebook, which is mostly for personal relationships. It can still be a great place to connect and inspire others who can relate to where you came from or where you are now. You can use LinkedIn, which is for professional connections. Promote professional projects on that platform, which this can segue into generating income or more. Twitter and Instagram are for short chats, mostly non-familiar connections. What I love about Twitter is how a tweet can go viral and hashtags trend. Also, people say that if you're in the technology arena, Twitter is the social media platform of choice. Instagram can be used to grow your audience, but the algorithms change periodically. (No, I don't have the cheat codes for any of the algorithms used on any of the social media platforms.) Regardless of which platform you decide, make sure you interact with your audience frequently. Respond to comments and direct messages. I encourage you to get more guidance on how to get more exposure on social media if you plan to use it. Social media is still a struggle for me.

In addition to social media, you can write a book or speak to an audience that will be encouraged by your message. I often struggle with what should come first: the book or speaking. Credibility is gained by writing a book, but I spoke to motivate small groups long before writing my first book. The only thing that really matters is that you're sharing your story from your heart, and you're connecting with people and inspiring them to challenge their beliefs about who they are and who they want to be. Experience is nice but not required. The only requirement is being passionate about your message. The enthusiasm from your passion will transform you into a people magnet. Inspiration is the highest form of success, and your passion will inspire people.

Another idea is to create a blog to share your story. Blogging is more of an exchange. Readers can comment and provide feedback on your topics. Also, they may want to work with you. As you learn how to create value for others with your humble brags, you'll inspire others. As you are on this part of your journey, remember how you can use that to network.

Networking is important as you inspire others. Once you get to a certain level of inspiring others, people will start to share your story. People will mention your name in rooms you have never stepped a foot in. How do you want people to mention your name? Think about what it is you want people to know about you. I feel passionate about teen parenting, closing the gap for others, people who struggle with procrastination, overwhelmed women, and mental health concerns. I want people to know that about me and feel confident about who they are no matter what barriers or obstacles they face on their journey. I want to be known for helping people find clarity in chaos.

Part of success is being prepared when you get the moment to inspire someone else. The journey has lots of turns and detours that involve delays and shortcuts. Everything that you do prepares you for your moment. Sometimes, the moment is a phone call, a visit, a request for you to sit on a board, a speaking opportunity, your opinion, or taking a different position. When I became a nurse manager, I had an a-ha moment. I knew I was the fifth African American and the third African American female in a nursing management role at that facility. I was excited to be in leadership and wanted to make myself proud. But more than that, I knew my performance would make it easier or harder for the next person who looks like me to get an opportunity. This was the same facility I experienced a racial incident in when I entered the building to apply for a nursing position. Because of my skin color, people assumed I was applying for a housekeeping position. Now, I am a bit of an overachiever, but it's only because I have high expectations for myself.

That leadership role gave birth to so many opportunities for me to inspire others. My direct reports, patients, doctors, administration, visitors, organizations, students, other disciplines of healthcare, and the list goes on. Indirectly and directly, I was shining a light on each element I identified with, including my race, nursing, teen pregnancy, womanhood, and parenthood. Those were the best ways for people to relate to me and see themselves. It was a natural spark to challenge how they feel about their best version. The idea of others being inspired by me inspired me. I was mindful of how I showed up every day—not physically but mentally. How you show up makes a difference. Being present and fully engaged are what gravitates people to you without you trying to get the attention of others. It's the same thing we previously covered when we discussed how your attitude is showing. Your attitude shows at every moment. It can attract people or make people run for the hills before they see you.

There was a nursing instructor who loved to scare the heck out of the nursing students. No one liked her and feared her class and clinicals. She was brutal, and it seemed as if she went out of her way to be mean and hurtful. She was a strong nurse but a horrible instructor. I remembered being humiliated at clinicals and being called superficial. I can take constructive criticism, but criticism that's not from a good place and only meant to tear another person down is uncalled for, especially in an educational setting. I didn't take it personally because she was consistently rude and ugly to all of the students. She was a master of negativity. My heart fluttered with joy when I no longer had to deal with her in nursing school, but it wasn't the last time I dealt with her. I discovered my first management position was hers before her firing. So, it turned out she wasn't as perfect as she thought. She's a good example of how people will do everything within their power to avoid you if you bring out the worse in them and leave a bad taste in their mouths.

I pray I have dropped enough pearls for you to lace a pearl necklace to wear along your journey to ultimate success. Each pearl will represent something you see with a different lens. Each pearl will provide clarity to what is trapping you, something you've been aware of but didn't have the courage or tools to nurture and set it free. The pearl necklace will be your confidence, resilience, and motivation to be fearless and never give up on what's destined to be yours.

When something's meant for you, nothing can threaten it. No obstacle will be big enough to stop you. No requirement will be able to prevent you from getting it. It's yours—all you have to do to keep going until you get it. I knew I was supposed to be a mother, wife, nurse, and entrepreneur. My answer to how I did the things I have accomplished is always "failure wasn't an option, so I never gave up." That's the only difference between those who crush their goals and those who do not. Keep trying until you get it done. There will be times you need to pivot but don't give up. In contrast, you don't want anything that isn't for you.

Imagine crushing your goals with confidence, motivation, and resilience. Try imaging not letting self-sabotaging thoughts distract you from being faithful and taking risks. If only you could see yourself as God sees you. Just in case no one has told you what my grandmother told me, "The sky's the limit." It really is the limit. That means you can have enormous goals and visions with no limit. There are things you can do that haven't formed in your mind. Someone is waiting on you to crush your goals. Now, go crush it! Be unstoppable!

About the Author

Jamesha Ross is an author, nursepreneur, app developer, inventor, and success coach who helps women shift their goals and visions into action so they can become their best version and inspire others.

Defying statistics, Jamesha overcame child abuse, teenage pregnancy at fourteen, gang violence at sixteen, and domestic violence. She is a wife and mother. Jamesha started her speaking career with church youth groups and students to motivate and discover purpose. She enjoys inspiring teens and women to achieve their purpose-driven goals and end the habit of procrastination.

In the past fifteen years, she has helped countless women crush their goals. She lives in Oklahoma with her husband and children.

Connect with her at JameshaRossRN.com

Notes

1. Steve Jobs. "Steve Jobs' 2005 Stanford Commencement Address." Stanford University Commencement, Stanford University, filmed June 12, 2005. Video of speech, 15:04: https://www.youtube.com/watch?v=UF8uR6Z6KLc/.
2. Elizabeth Hopper. "Maslow's Hierarchy of Needs Explained." ThoughtCo. February 24, 2020. https://www.thoughtco.com/maslows-hierarchy-of-needs-4582571/.
3. Michael Todd. Crazy Faith: It's Only Crazy Until It Happens. Colorado Springs: WaterBrook, 2021.
4. Rory Vaden. "Take the Stairs." Speech, Tulsa, OK, February 23, 2012.
5. myplate.gov
6. https://medium.com/the-post-grad-survival-guide/actionable-steps-to-building-7-income-streams-like-a-millionaire-9ed11c59630c

www.ingramcontent.com/pod-product-compliance
Lightning Source LLC
LaVergne TN
LVHW051952060526
838201LV00059B/3610